TZITZITH
A THREAD OF LIGHT

TZITZITH
A THREAD OF LIGHT
ARYEH KAPLAN

NCSY/Orthodox Union

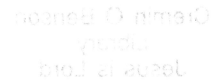

Published by the National Conference of Synagogue Youth/Union of Orthodox Jewish Congregations of America, 333 Seventh Avenue, New York, NY 10001.

Distributed in Israel by Mesorah Mafitzim
J. Grossman, 117 Rechov Uziel, Jerusalem.

ISBN 1-879016-03-6

PRINTED IN THE UNITED STATES OF AMERICA

This Sefer is dedicated
to the memory of
Abel and Eva Refson
by their children
Rabbis Dovid and Yehuda Refson

A Publication

in the

JOSEPH TANENBAUM LIBRARY
Series

CONTENTS

INTRODUCTION
by Rabbi Pinchas Stolper

How can we learn to control our passions so that we will rule over them, and not allow them to rule over us? How are we to avoid the self-deception which so often tells us that truth and beauty are synonymous, and that human fulfillment and physical pleasures are one and the same thing?

The Torah wants us to arrive at the conclusion that discipline and self-control are the key to human happiness. It gives us the tools with which to prevent our eyes and our hearts from enticing us into thinking that life is the pursuit of pleasure—the pursuit of beauty, and physical things. The Torah wants to keep us from traveling the wrong road on which we will find suffering, frustration, evil and the suppression of our highest and most noble aspirations.

Our Sages teach us that, "He who carefully observes the commandment of Tzitzith will be able to behold the 'Face' of the All-Present God" (Menachoth 436), because God does not want us to "explore after our heart and after our eyes, after which we go astray". As Rashi says, "The eye sees, then the heart

x   Tzitzith—A Thread of Light

desires, and then the body sins." But God does not want us to be misled by our eyes and our hearts—therefore, he has given us a visible reminder of Himself and His Laws. Tzitzith, which means to *"appear in visible form"* (Hirsch), remind us that the animal in us seeks gratification only from physical things which can be seen and felt, while our truest, greatest and most meaningful attainments and relationships are with or from God who is unseen and invisible.

The Tzitzith and the Tallith are reminders of the fact that clothes are the first visible characteristic which distinguish man from the animal—clothes remind us of the need to conceal the animal in ourselves and be constantly aware of the invisible God and His commands.

In this deep and moving book Rabbi Aryeh Kaplan has again taken us beyond simple and superficial meanings. Here, he delves deeply into the mystery of the commandment of Tzitzith to reveal the link between Tzitzith, the sin of the first man, and the ability of mankind to overcome sin and reach toward God. Here we are introduced to an understanding of the connection between clothes, the sexual urge, self-control and the story of the serpent. Here we begin to realize that God has instilled within us the ability to choose freely so that we will not function as mindless robots. Instead, we have within us the ability to overcome evil and gain mastery over ourselves in order to create a new world in which mankind will rule his instincts, overcome the beast in himself, and create a society of the spirit in which good and truth will prevail and in which war, hatred and evil will be banished forever.

TZITZITH
A THREAD OF LIGHT

WHY TZITZITH?

Have you ever thought about the really important questions in life? Have you ever asked yourself why you were born? What is the purpose of life? What are your responsibilities? Have you ever tried to develop a philosophy of life and then live by it? One of the world's greatest philosophers came to the conclusion that "the unexamined life is not worth living."[4] Have you ever examined *your* life?

Of course, we all know the main problem is not so much developing a philosophy of life, but living up to it. If we think, we know what is right and what is wrong. But when it comes down to the crunch, we tend to forget.

Deep down, every Jew realizes that Judaism offers a philosophy of life that is without equal. One does not have to be overly sophisticated to realize that a philosophy of life that has survived for over three thousand years, and has dealt with every possible human problem in every possible society, must have an overriding

---

[4] Socrates, in Plato's *Phaedo*.

validity. Looking at it that way, the fact that it originated with God seems almost perfectly obvious.

Yet, in the heat of everyday life, there are many
things that draw us away from God and Judaism. There
are friends who pull us to conform, good times that
beckon, and a desirable world of pleasures that tempts
us away, even from the truths that we recognize. Above
all, there is the strong itch of desire that sweeps us
along, often against our very will.

We may know what is right, but there are so many
things that make us forget. It is so very hard to remember.

God realized this, so He gave us a commandment to
serve as a constant reminder. The Torah clearly spells
this out when it says, "They shall be your Tzitzith, and
you shall see them and remember all of God's commandments and obey them, and not stray after your
heart and eyes, which lead you to immorality."

In the simplest sense, then, the Tzitzith serve as a
reminder. We bind them to our garments just as one
might tie a string around his finger[5] or belt[6] in order to
remember something. Some say that the Tzitzith is reminiscent of a lash,[7] serving to remind us that we are ultimately accountable for all our deeds and misdeeds.[8] We
wear them as a constant reminder that we must obey
God's commandments, and not be led astray by our
desires.

---

[5] Alshech on Numbers 15:39.
[6] *Tur Orach Chaim* 24.
[7] *Zohar* 1:175a; Bach, *Orach Chaim* 24, s.v. *Tzitzith*.
[8] *Menachoth* 44a; Rashi on Numbers 15:40; *Reshith Chochmah, Shaar
HaKedushah* 6 (141c); *Pri Etz Chaim, Shaar Tzitzith*, note #1 (Ashlag, 5526)
p. 81; *Likutey Moharan* 7:4. *Cf. Tikuney Zohar* 18 (37a).

This is also apparent from the context in which the commandment was given. Immediately before God gave the commandment of Tzitzith, the Torah tells of a man who committed a most serious sin. The Midrash explains that God then taught Moses that this man had sinned "because he did not have anything to remind him constantly of his responsibility." In response to this, He gave the commandment of Tzitzith.[9]

Along with this immediate benefit, the Torah also tells us of a long-term effect.[10] Here God speaks to us directly, "In order that you remember and keep all My commandments, and be holy to your God." That is, if we allow the Tzitzith to be a constant reminder, keeping us from being misled by worldly temptations, we will form the habit of remembering God's commandments. This in turn will ultimately lead us to become holy; that is, immersed in the Godly, rather than in our worldly desires.[11]

The commandment ends with a mention of the Exodus from Egypt: "I am God your Lord who brought you out of the land of Egypt, to be your God—I am God your Lord."

One thing the Torah is telling us here is why the commandment of Tzitzith, as well as the other commandments, were given to the Jews in particular, and not to all people. There is a special bond between God and the Jew which was forged at the Exodus. God here says, "I

---

[9] *Tanna DeBei Eliahu Rabbah* 26 (104a); Ramban, *Baaley Tosafoth*, on Numbers 15:32. The Abarbanel, however, writes that this was one of the first commandments given to the Jews.

[10] Abarbanel on Numbers 15:40 (86b); Alshech *ibid*.

[11] *Sifri* (115), Malbim, *Or HaChaim*, on Numbers 15:40; *Reshith Chochmah, Shaar HaKedushah* 6 (141a).

... brought you out of Egypt to be your God." The unique miracles of the Exodus had this specific purpose—to forge this bond between God and Israel. God therefore repeats, "I am God your Lord"—now and forever.[12]

The Exodus was a unique event in the annals of history. It was the only time that God ever revealed Himself to an entire people, literally changing the course of both nature and history. The Torah therefore asks us, "Did God ever venture to take a nation for Himself, from the midst of another nation, with a challenge, with signs and wonders, as God your Lord did in Egypt before your very eyes? You have had sure proof that God is the Lord; there is no other" (*Deuteronomy 4:34*). The Exodus made every Jew uniquely aware of God and showed Him to be profoundly involved in the affairs of man.[13]

The Exodus and events surrounding it made Judaism unique among religions. Other faiths began with a single individual who claimed to have a special message. He gradually gathered a following and his disciples converted others, creating a new religion. This is the pattern followed by almost every great world religion.

The only exception to this is Judaism. God brought the entire Jewish people out of Egypt, and ultimately brought them to the foot of Mount Sinai where they all heard His message. It is most interesting to note that the very first words of the Ten Commandments are, "I am God your Lord who brought you out of the land of Egypt, from the house of slavery" (*Exodus 20:2, Deute-*

---

[12] *Cf. Sifri* (115), Rashi, Malbim, on Numbers 15:41; *Zohar* 3:176a.
[13] *Kuzari* 1:89; *Yad, Yesodey HaTorah* 8:1; *Moreh Nevukhim* 2:35.

ronomy 5:6). This was both the culmination and the realization of the drama of the Exodus.

It is because of the unique bond forged at the Exodus that the Jew in particular must keep the commandments of the Torah. Through the commandments, this bond is strengthened and renewed, preserving the Jew and maintaining him on a high spiritual level. God therefore tells us, "I am God your Lord, who brought you out of the land of Egypt, and you shall observe all of My rules and laws and keep them—I am God" (*Leviticus 19:36,37*).

The Exodus thus places a very special responsibility on the Jew. God rescued us from slavery, and in a very special sense, became our Master. In the Torah He says, "The children of Israel are My servants, whom I brought forth out of the land of Egypt—I am God your Lord" (*Leviticus 25:25*).

Therefore, in a sense, the Tzitzith are an insignia that we wear, proclaiming that we are God's subjects.[14] It is because of the Exodus that we are God's subjects in this very special way.

The Torah alludes to this in telling us to wear Tzitzith to be "holy to your God." The word "holy" means two things: First that we are close to God; and second, that we are separated from things that are ungodly.[15] We wear Tzitzith as a sign of our special relationship with God, as the ones who accepted His Torah. God reiterates the concept of this relationship when He says,

---

[14] *Menachoth* 43b, Rashi, *Tosafoth ad loc.* s.v. *Choshen, Pesikta Zutratha.* Sforno, Abarbanel, *Or HaChaim* on Numbers 15:39. Bachya *ibid.* quoting *Bahir* 93; *Sefer Ha-Chinukh* 386; *Zohar* 3:174b; *Etz Chaim, Shaar HaShemoth* 7 (p. 343); *Derekh Hashem* 4:6:6.

[15] See *Tosafoth, Kiddushin* 2b s.v. *DeAsar.*

"You shall be holy to Me, for I, God, am Holy, and I have set you apart from all other peoples, that you should be Mine" (*Leviticus 20:26*).

But we must understand the reason for all this. Why are the Jews so unique? Why did God have to choose a particular group of people as His own special servants? Why, in short, are the Jews the "chosen people"?

God needed a special group of people who would undertake to lead the rest of humanity and show them the way. Looking at the generations before Abraham, God saw that humanity as a whole could not maintain a high moral and spiritual level. He therefore chose Abraham and his children, the Jews, as His special representatives, to proclaim His teachings to all the world. This is what God told us through His prophet, "I, God, have called you in righteousness . . . and have set you as a covenant of the people, as a light for the nations" (*Isaiah 42:6*). Israel's special mission is to bear witness to God, as we again find, "You are My witnesses," says God, "and My servants, whom I have chosen" (*Isaiah 43:10*).[16]

Although the Jew constantly fulfills this mission, the main time of its fruition will be in the Messianic Age. When all Jews are brought back to God by the Messiah (*Mashiach*), they in turn will influence all mankind in this direction. This is one of the main prophecies of the Messianic Age (*Isaiah 2:2–4*):

> It shall come to pass in the end of days
>> that the mountain of God's house
>>> shall be set over all other mountains

---

[16] These passages refer either to Israel or to the Messiah. In either case, the enlightenment of all peoples will be through Israel.

and lifted high above the hills
and all nations shall come streaming to it.
Many people shall come and say:
Come, let us go up to God's mountain
to the house of Israel's God
and He will teach us His ways
and we will walk in His paths.
For out of Zion shall go forth the Torah
and God's word from Jerusalem.
And He will judge between nations
and decide between peoples.
And they will beat their swords into plowshares
and their spears into pruning hooks.
Nation shall not lift up sword against nation
neither will they practice war anymore.

From this we learn that the Jews will be in a unique position of moral leadership in the Messianic Age. But who among the Jews will be in a position to exert such leadership? Who will be the ones deemed capable of spreading God's word to the rest of the world?

Our sages teach us that it will be those individuals who are careful to observe the commandment of Tzitzith. Regarding this, the prophet foretold, "In those days, ten men of each language will grasp the corner of [a garment containing Tzitzith, worn by] a Jewish man, and they will say, 'Let us go with you for we have heard that God is with you'" (*Zechariah 8:23*).[17]

---

[17] *Shabbath* 32b; *Sifri*, Bachya (83b); *Etz Chaim*, loc. cit.; *Likutey Halachoth*, Tzitzith 3:9 (38a).

WHAT ARE TZITZITH?

[This chapter is somewhat technical, and may be skipped on the first reading.]

If you have ever worn a Tallith or *Tallith Katan*, you are probably aware of the Tzitzith or tassels hanging on each of the four corners. If you look more carefully you will see that they are made of eight strings, or more accurately, four strings doubled over to make eight. You will also notice that they are attached through a small hole near the corner and that they contain five knots and four groups of windings between the knots.

If you take the trouble to count the windings, you will see that the group nearest the corner has seven windings, the next, eight, the next eleven, and the last one, thirteen. (See figure 1)

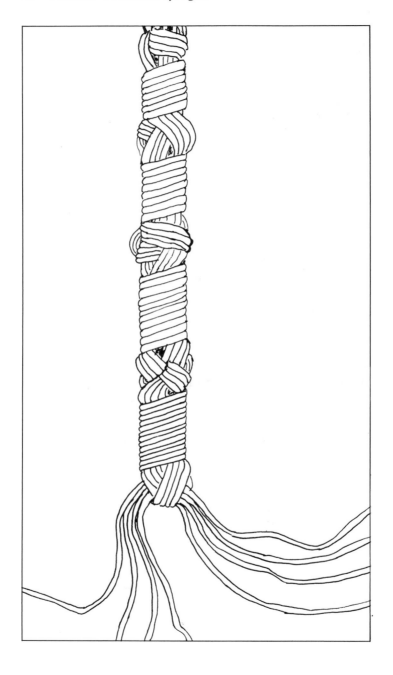

Look closely at the individual strings, and you will notice that they are each made of two threads, tightly twisted together.

All this shows that Tzitzith are more than simple strings. There are set rules as to how they must be made, and each of these rules has a reason. We must first explore how these rules are derived from the Torah, and then delve more deeply into their significance. We will discover that they are not mere strings, that Tzitzith touch upon some of the deepest philosophical concepts of Judaism.

Before going into the rules of Tzitzith, it would be useful to review the two places where they are mentioned in the Torah. The first, which we have already quoted is (*Numbers 15:38*):

> Speak to the sons of Israel and say to them that they make Tzitzith on the corners of their garments for [all] generations; and they shall place on the corner Tzitzith a twist (*Pethil*) of blue [wool].

The second reference is (*Deuteronomy 22:11,12*):

> You shall not wear *Shaatnez* (a mixture of) linen and wool together.
> [But] you shall make tassels (*Gedilim*) on the four corners of your garments, with which you cover yourself.

First we must define the terms used by the Torah. There are three basic words that need definition: Tzitzith, *Pethil*, and *Gedilim*.

The word Tzitzith only occurs in one other place in the Bible, where we find, "The form of a hand came forth, and I was grasped by a lock of hair (*Tzitzith*) on my head" (*Ezekiel 8:3*). Referring to this verse, the Talmud tells us that Tzitzith are a group of freely hanging strings, resembling a lock of hair.[18] We thus have the first requirement of Tzitzith: They must contain a number of loose strings. This part of the Tzitzith is called the *Anaf.*

The Torah then tells us, "You shall place on the corner Tzitzith a twist (*Pethil*) of blue [wool]." We will discuss the question of the blue in a separate section, but the word *Pethil* or "twist" has a very special significance. It means a "twisted string," but it also has three other connotations:

The first connotation of the word *Pethil* is that of a winding; from this we derive the fact that one of the strings must be wound around the rest.[19] The Torah therefore states that it should be placed "*on* the corner Tzitzith." The Tzitzith refer to the loose threads and the *Pesil* or winding is placed over and around them. The threads are first hung to form loose strings or Tzitzith. Then we take another string and wind it "on" them. In ancient times, when the blue thread was still used, it

---

[18] *Menachoth* 42a; *Sifri*, Rashi, *loc. cit.*; *Tosafoth*, *Menachoth* 39b s.v. *O'Gedil*, *Yad*, *Tzitzith* 1:1. According to the second explanation in Rashi, *Menachoth* 39b s.v. *U'Poslehah*, however, we derive this from the word *Pesil*. Also see *Tosafoth ibid. U'Poslehah*, *Shita Mekubetzeth* #1; *Nimukey Yosef* (*Rif*, *Hilchoth Tzitzith* 12b) s.v. *Anaf*. Also see Rashi on Numbers 15:38; *Sifethey Chachamim ad loc.* #5; *Rashbam, ibid.* For a deeper reason for this, see *Zohar* 3:174b; *Etz Chaim, Shaar HaChashmal* 3; *Shaar HaKavanoth, Tzitzith* 2 (p. 27); *Pri Etz Chaim, Tzitzith;* 3 (p. 67); *Likutey Moharan* 8:8.

[19] Rashi, *Menachoth* 39b s.v. *U'Poslehah*, in first explanation; *Tosafoth Ibid. "U'Poslehah"*; Rashi on Deuteronomy 32:5; *Yad, Tzitzith* 1:2,3, *P'er HaDor* (*Tshuvoth Rambam*) 21, 47, quoted in *Kesef Mishneh Tzitzith* 1:7; *Zohar* 3:175a; *Pesil Techeleth* 7 (p. 147). See note 25.

was the string used to make most of the winding.

The second connotation is that of two threads twisted together.[20] This is one reason why each of the Tzitzith strings is made out of two threads twisted together like a rope. Most authorities also agree that whenever a string is mentioned in Jewish law, it is always defined as one twisted out of two or more threads. Tzitzith follow this rule.[21]

The third connotation of the word *Pethil* is almost a combination of the first two. The word means both "joined" and "bent," and therefore, it also denotes a doubled string. From this we learn that the strings are doubled. This is the reason we make the Tzitzith out of four strings, and then double them over to make eight.[22] We find a number of other places where a blue thread was used, such as in the priestly garments; there, too, it was placed through a hole and doubled over.[23]

---

[20] Sifri, Targum Yonathan, Malbim *ad loc.*; *Tosafoth, Yebamoth* 4b s.v. *VeAmar.* Also see *Orach Chaim* 11:2; *Turey Zahav ad loc.* 11:2; *Eruvin* 96b, *Rokeach* 361 (p. 246). The word *Pesil* has the connotation of two things bound together, as we find in Rashi on Numbers 19:15; Genesis 39:8. The Rambam, however, does not require this, *cf. Yad, Tzitzith* 1:10, *Kesef Mishneh ad loc.; P'er HaDor* 22; *Chatham Sofer* on *Orach Chaim* 11:2.

[21] This is true of the threads used to weave the priestly garments, and Raavad, *Tzitzith* 1:10 derives this requirement in the case of *Tzitzith* from this fact. *Cf. Yoma* 71b. It is also true with regard to the Biblical prohibition of *Shaatnez,* and this also relates to *Tzitzith,* see *Tosafoth, Menachoth* 39b s.v. *Kesher, Nidah* 61b s.v. *Shua;* Ran, *Betza* (Rif 7b) s.v. *MiDeOraitha.*

[22] *Tosafoth, Menachoth* 38a s.v. *HaTecheleth,* end; *Ibid.* 39b s.v. *U'Poslehah, Yebamoth* 5b s.v. *U'Poslehah.* See *Shabbath* 2:3 (28b), Rashi *ad loc.* s.v. *SheKifluha; Betza* 32b. *Cf. Menachoth* 42a, *Yad, Tzitzith* 1:6; *Orach Chaim* 11:12. The *Levush* (*HaTecheleth* 11:4), however, writes that this is the most logical way to attach the Tzitzith, and that the derivation from the word *Pesil* is merely an allusion.

[23] See Rashi on Exodus 28:37, 39:31; *Yad, Kley HaMikdash* 9:2. *Cf. Yoma* 72a, according to *Tosafoth, Menachoth* 38a s.v. *HaTecheleth.*

Finally, the Torah says, "You shall make *Gedilim* (tassels) on the four corners of your garment." This immediately tells us that Tzitzith are only worn on a four-cornered or rectangular garment. This is why both the Tallith and *Tallith Katan* are rectangular in shape.[24]

The word *Gedilim* itself teaches us another important fact about the Tzitzith. Whereas the word Tzitzith refers to loose hairs or strings, the word *Gedil* means hair or strings bound together to form a tassel, braid or rope.[25] Obviously, a single string, even if doubled and twisted, would not be called a *Gedil* or tassel. (As we have already seen, the word *Pesil* already has this connotation.) It must therefore refer to a minimum of two doubled strings. The word used in the Torah—*Gedilim*—is plural; therefore, there must be a "doubled tassel" in each corner. This is an allusion to the fact that the Tzitzith must contain four doubled strings. *Gedil* in singular is two, and *Gedilim* in plural is four.[26] Of

[24] *Menachoth* 43a; *Zevachim* 18b; *Sifri* (234) on Deuteronomy 22:12; *Yad, Tzitzith* 3:1; *Orach Chaim* 10:1.

[25] *Sifri* (115) on Numbers 15:38, (234) on Deuteronomy 22:12; *Tosafoth, Menachoth* 41a s.v. *Beth Shamai; Nimukey Yosef, Hilchoth Tzitzith* (Rif 12b) s.v. *Tanya;* Rosh, *Hilkhoth Tzitzith* 12; *Baal Ha Turim* on Deuteronomy 22:12. See 1 Kings 7:17; *Targum* on Exodus 28:14, 22, 24, 39:15, Judges 15:13, Isaiah 5:18; *Gittin* 69a; *Betza* 32b; Bertenoro on *Shabbath* 10:6. There is, however, another opinion that maintains that the word *Gedil* refers to the windings, see Rashi, *Menachoth* 39b s.v. *U'Poslehah,* second explanation, 39a s.v. *Chut, Yebamoth* 5b s.v.*U'Poslehah.* For the difficulties with this explanation, see *Tosafoth, Menachoth* 3b *O Gedil,* s.v. *U'Poslehah.*

[26] *Menachoth* 39b; *Yebamoth* 5b; Rashi, *Menachoth* 42a s.v. *KeDidan, Sanhedrin* 89b s.v. *U'Perusho, Yoma* 72a s.v. *Kelil.* According to this opinion, the reference is to the four strings before they are doubled. Another opinion, however, holds that it refers to the strings after they are doubled, and only to the white strings. Since there are an equal number of blue strings according to this view, the total number is eight. See *Tosafoth, Bechoroth* 39b s.v. *Kama, Menachoth* 38a, s.v. *HaTecheleth* 41b s.v. *Bais Shamai.*

course, aside from this allusion, this is also known from tradition.[27]

Recapitulating, we now see that the Tzitzith have two basic parts. The first part consists of loose strings, alluded to in the word Tzitzith. This is called the *Anaf.* The second part consists of the upper section, where the strings are tied together with the winding. This is called the *Gedil.* For aesthetic reasons, our sages decreed that the *Gedil* consist of one third of the length of the entire Tzitzith, and the *Anaf* the other two-thirds.[28]

The Knots

The derivation of the knots in the Tzitzith involves a number of interesting concepts. Basically, the fact that the Tzitzith must be knotted to the garment is known from oral tradition, as handed down from the time of Moses.[29]

There is, however, an important allusion to be found in the Torah. In the Biblical quotation which refers to *Gedilim,* you will notice that the commandment for Tzitzith comes right after the prohibition against *Shaatnez.* The laws of *Shaatnez* are fairly well known. Most of us are aware that the Torah forbids us to wear any

---

[27] *Sanhedrin* 89a; *Kesef Mishneh, Tzitzith* 1:1, *Sefer HaKobets, ibid.;* *Beth Yosef, Orach Chaim* 11 (16b) s.v. *U'R. Y. Cf. Sefer HaMitvoth, Shoresh* 2; *Magid Mishneh, Kesef Mishneh, Ishuth* 1:2.

[28] *Menachoth* 39a; *Yad, Tzitzith* 1:8; *Orach Chaim* 11:14 in *Hagah.* If this requirement is not met, the Tzitzith are still valid, Maharshal on *Sefer Mitzvoth Gadol* (Smag), positive commandment 26; *Turey Zahav* 11:15. In *Chayay Adam* 11:19, however, we find an opinion that this is actually a Rabbinical law.

[29] Rashi, *Menachoth* 39a s.v. *Kesher, Tosafoth Yeshenim, Yebamoth* 4b s.v. *A. Avel.*

garment containing both wool and linen. Even today, we must be careful of this, since many woolen garments, especially men's suits, contain linen as a stiffener in the lining or collar. Linen thread is also used occasionally to sew on buttons, and this must be replaced before a woolen suit can be worn. A network of "Shaatnez Laboratories" exists, whose sole purpose is to examine garments and ascertain that they do not contain *Shaatnez.* Many major clothing chains will send garments to these laboratories for free testing and rectification where necessary.

Everything in the Torah has a reason, even its order, so the fact that the commandment of *Shaatnez* is right next to that of Tzitzith comes to teach us something. According to Talmudic tradition, the laws of *Shaatnez* are set aside when one must place the blue woolen Tzitzith thread in a linen Tallith. The juxtaposition of the two commandments comes specifically to teach us this exception.[30] This was, however, only true when the blue thread was still in use.[31]

We must now take into account still another rule, that the prohibition of *Shaatnez* only applies when the linen and wool are permanently attached together. Thus, the very tradition that the commandment of Tzitzith can override that of *Shaatnez,* teaches us that the Tzitzith must be permanently attached to the garment. The simplest way of attaching the strings in a permanent way is by tying them on with a double knot.

Since this is a fairly complex argument, it is useful to see how it is presented in the Talmud:[32]

[30] *Yebamoth* 4a,b; *Sifri* (233) on Deuteronomy 22:11.
[31] *Tur Orach Chaim* 11 (17a); *Orach Chaim* 9:1.
[32] *Menachoth* 39a. Cf. *Sanhedrin* 89a.

Rabba said: We thus learn that the upper knot is Biblical in origin (*DeOraitha*).

For if we were to say that it is only of Rabbinical origin (*DeRabanan*), why must the Torah permit the use of [woolen] Tzitzith on a linen garment?

It would obviously be [permitted, since the two are not permanently attached], and a single knot is not considered a [permanent] attachment.

We therefore see that it is Biblical in origin.

According to most commentaries, this "upper knot" refers to the double knot at the end of the windings.[33] According to this interpretation, this knot is also necessary to hold the windings in place. Unless knotted at the end, the windings would not be a permanent, integral part of the Tzitzith.[34]

Therefore, according to the primary law, the Tzitzith only require one double knot at the end of the windings. Some authorities also require a knot near the corner, before the windings. According to this opinion,

---

[33] Rashi, *Menachoth* 39a s.v. *Kesher, Tosafoth ibid.*; *Smag*, positive 26; *Magen Avraham* 11:19; *Turey Zahav* 11:14; *Mishneh Berurah* 11:64; HaGra on *Orach Chaim* 11:13. Others, however, interpret this to refer to the knot nearest the Tallith, see Rashi, *Sanhedrin* 88a s.v. *Kesher, Shitah Mekubetzeth, Menachoth* 39a #6; *Tosafoth ibid.* s.v. *Kesher, Levush (HaTecheleth)* 11:14. Rashi states that there is a dispute as to whether or not this knot is actually required by the Torah (*DeOraitha*) see *Tosafoth, Sanhedrin* 89a s.v. *Kesher, Chidushey HaRan ibid.* According to the Rambam, *Yad Tzitzith* 1:2, it would appear that this knot is not required, but see *Beth Yosef, Orach Chaim* 11 (17a) s.v. *VaYikach.*

[34] *Tosafoth, Menachoth* 39a s.v. *Kesher.* The majority opinion is that the knot is tied with four strings on either side as we do it. Rabenu Tam, however, would tie the knots with the string used in the windings opposite the seven others. See *Shitah Mekubetzeth, Menachoth* 39a #13 end; Rosh, *Hilkhoth Tzitzith* 15, *Maadney Yom Tov ad loc.* #20; *Diverey Chamudos ibid.* 20; *Mordecai, Hilkhoth Tzitzith* 940 (1d); *Beth Yosef, Orach Chaim* 11 (17a) s.v. *U'Kathuv, Perisha ibid.* 11:17.

the Tzitzith must have at least two knots, one before, and one after the windings.[35]

It is a most ancient custom to include five knots in Tzitzith.[36]

There are many reasons given for this custom. Some say that they are meant to represent the five books of the Torah: Genesis (*Bereishith*), Exodus (*Shemos*), Leviticus (*VaYikra*), Numbers (*BeMidbar*), and Deuteronomy (*Devarim*). In this manner, the Tzitzith recall "all of God's commandments."[37]

Others say that the five knots are reminiscent of the five senses, indicating that they all must be dedicated to God.[38]

Still another source indicates that they represent the first five words of the *Sh'ma: Sh'ma Yisrael Adonoy Elohenu Adonoy*—"Hear O Israel, God is our Lord, God is . . ." The final word, *Echad*—One—is then indicated by the windings, which bind all the threads together into *one* unit.[39] A number of other reasons are also given; they will be discussed later.[40]

The Torah does not specify the number of windings required in the Tzitzith. All that is required is a single

[35] *Shitah Mekubetzeth, Menachoth* 38a #6, *Nimukey Yosef, Hilkhoth Tzitzith* (Rif 12b) s.v. *Keshara DeYaved; Kesef Mishneh, Tzitzith* 1:9 end; HaGra, *Orach Chaim* 11:13 s.v. *Shelm, Mishneh Berurah* 11:64.

[36] See *Targum Yonathan* on Numbers 15:38.

[37] *Zohar* 3:228a; *Baal HaTurim* on Numbers 15:38; *Tur Orach Chaim* 24; *Orach Chaim* 24:1.

[38] Bachya on Numbers 15:38 (83a).

[39] *Tikuney Zohar* 10 (25b). Cf. *Menachoth* 43b, that the commandment of Tzitzith is supposed to remind us of the Sh'ma.

[40] According to Rashi, the reason for the custom of five knots was so that together with the eight strings and the numerical value of Tzitzith, it should add up to 613. See below, part 2, note 75; *Rashi, Menachoth* 39a s.v. *Min, Shitah Mekubetzeth* #10; *Tosafoth bid. s.v. Lo. Tosafoth* also presents an

triplet (*Chulya*), consisting of three windings.[41] Indeed, in a dire emergency, one may make such minimal Tzitzith, tying a double knot, making the three windings, and then tying another double knot.[42]

Rabbinical law, however, requires that one-third of the Tzitzith consist of windings, and the other two-thirds of the loose strings, as discussed earlier. Since it is the custom to have five double knots in the Tzitzith, there are four groups of windings separating the knots. The accepted practice is for the first group to be made with seven windings, the second with eight, the third with eleven, and the fourth with thirteen. We will discuss the reason for this custom in a later section.[43]

There are a number of other laws regarding Tzitzith that bear mentioning. First of all, one cannot make Tzitzith out of just any strings. They must be made either of wool or of exactly the same material as the Tallith. They must also be spun especially to be used in Tzitzith. This is true even of the two strings that are twisted together to make each cord. In this respect, Tzitzith are no different from any other ritual object that must be made specifically for its intended ritual purpose.[44]

---

opinion that the five knots were actually required because of the blue. Three of the four groups of windings consisted of a triplet of white combined with one of blue, while the fourth one was a triplet of white alone. The four groups were thus composed of the seven triplets required by Talmudic law. Since each group was fastened on both sides by a knot, the Tzitzith automatically contained five knots.

[41] *Menachoth* 39a, *Yad, Tzitzith* 1:9.

[42] *Magen Avraham* 11:19; *Mishneh Berurah* 11:66. The additional windings, however, must be completed as soon as possible, in order to fulfill the requirement that they comprise one third of the Tzitzith.

[43] *Orach Chaim* 11:14; *Magen Avraham* 11:22. See below, part 2, note 77.

[44] *Menachoth* 42a; *Orach Chaim* 11:1.

Measurements

There is another group of rules involving the dimensions of the Tzitzith and the measurements associated with them. Before beginning to explain them, however, there are several general concepts that must be understood.

In many places where the Torah requires something to be used for a ritual purpose, a certain measure or *Shiur* is required. These measures are known from the Oral Torah, which was transmitted from master to disciple from the time of Moses, and finally set in writing in the Talmud. Thus, when the Torah requires us to eat something (such as Matzah on Passover), we must eat a piece at least as large as an olive. This is the measure or *Shiur* for something to have the status of food. In the case of a beverage, the measure is a *Revi'ith*, approximately three fluid ounces. With regard to Tzitzith, we will discuss the measures involved in such things as cloth and thread.

All Talmudic measurements of length are presented in terms of a "finger" or *Agudel*, the width of an average thumb. There is some question as to the precise length of a "finger," but the majority of authorities agree that it lies somewhere between ¾ inch and one inch.[45]

___

[45] This is the equavelent to the length of six barleycorns laid side by side, or two, end to end. *Yad, Sefer Torah* 9:9. Various opinions of the length of a "finger" are: .787 in. or 2 cm. (*Misgereth HaShulchan HaSefardi, Chabad*); .866 in. or 2.2 cm. (*Chalath Aaron*, end); .935 in. or 2.375 cm. (*T'shuvoth Meshiv Davar* 24); .952 in. or 2.417 cm. (*Kitzur Shulchan Aruch*); .959–984 in. or 2.437–2.5 cm. (*T'shuvoth Imrey Yosher* 88) 1.033 in. or 2.625 cm. (*Darkey T'shuvah*); 1.036 in. or 2.632 cm. (*Toldoth Sh'muel*); 1.082 in. or 2.75 cm. (*Levush Malchuth*, according to *Chatham Sofer*). See *Shulchan Melachim*, p. 7a.

Other measurements are then defined in terms of this "finger." Those most often used are:

Agudel	"finger"		¾ inch-1 inch
Tefach	handbreadth	4 "fingers"	3-4 inches
Amah	cubit	6 handbreadths	18-24 inches

Making use of these measurements, we can discuss the measure used in cloth and thread.

A piece of woven material does not have the status of cloth unless it measures at least three "fingers" square, that is, three "fingers" by three "fingers."[46] Anything less than this is considered a useless scrap, and has no status in Jewish law.

In the case of thread or string, the measure is a "double span" or *Sit Kaful*, double the distance between the forefinger and middle finger when the hand is spread out. This is approximately equal to four "fingers" in length.[47] Anything less than this is also considered a useless scrap, and has no status in Jewish law. Therefore, in order for a piece of string or thread to have any ritual status, it must be at least four "fingers" long.

There is, however, one exception to this rule. The measure of a piece of string that is part of a garment is a

---

[46] *Kelim* 27:2; *Shabbath* 26b, 79a; *Yad, Kelim* 22:1, *Shabbath* 18:13.

[47] This is a "double span," or *Sit Kaful; Shabbath* 13:4 (105b), *Tosefta* 10:2. According to Rashi (*Ibid.* 106a), this is the distance between the thumb and forefinger when extended. Many authorities maintain that the single "span" or *Sit* is two fingers. See Rambam on *Orlah* 3:2, *Shabbath* 13:4, *Kelim* 13:4, *Shiltey Giborim, Shabbath* (Rif 38a) #2; Rav Hai Gaon, *Kelim* 13:4; *Aruch Sit*. This would make the "double span" equal to four fingers, or a single handbreadth. Another opinion, however, states that a span or *Sit* is two handbreadths, and a double span, four. See *Yad, Shabbath* 9:7, 10, 13, 15, 18:13; HaGra on *Orlah* 3:2.

"single span" or *Sit.* This equals two "fingers." When a piece of thread is part of a garment, it must be taken into account even if it is only two "fingers" long.[48]

Keeping all this in mind, we can now understand some of the measurements involving Tzitzith.

First of all, each part of the Tzitzith must contain a significant length of string. The shortest such section is the *Gedil* or wound section, which must therefore be at least four fingers long.

As discussed earlier, the wound portion or *Gedil* must comprise one-third of the length of the entire Tzitzith. Therefore, their entire length must be at least 12 fingers.[49]

From this, we see that the length of the Tzitzith must be between 9 and 12 inches. We usually take the stricter view and require them to be a foot long.

The question still remains as to where on the garment the Tzitzith must be hung. The Torah simply tells us to place them "on the corner," but no exact distance is given. This distance is derived from the general laws regarding cloth and thread.

The Torah tells us to place the Tzitzith"*on* the corners of your garments." The Talmud interprets the word "on" to mean that a significant portion of the Tzitzith must actually be "*on* the corner," that is, in contact with it.[50] The Talmud states that this portion must be

[48] *Orlah* 3:2,3.

[49] *Tosafoth, Menachoth* 41b s.v. *Bais Shamai, Bechoroth* 39b s.v. *Kama,* Rashi ibid. s.v. *Achath, Orach Chaim* 11:4. Others, however, hold that the entire Tzitzith need be only four fingers long, Rashi, *Menachoth* 41b s.v. *Meshulasheth; Yad, Tzitzith* 1:6. The *Levush* (*HaTecheleth*) 12, 1, 3, maintains that the entire requirement of any length is only based on Rabbinical law. Also see *Chayay Adam* 11:16.

[50] *Menachoth* 42a; Rashi *ad loc.* s.v. *SheTehey, Shitah Mekubetzeth ibid.* #5; *Radal ad loc.; Hagahoth Maimoni, Tzitzith* 1:6 #2, HaGra on *Orach Chaim* 11:9 *MiShum.* There are, however, a number of other interpretations to this statement.

the length of a "thumb joint" or *Kesher Agudel,* a measure which is approximately two fingers.[51] The hole through which the Tzitzith string is attached must therefore be at least two fingers from the edge of the garment.

The reason for this is obvious. As mentioned earlier, when a string or thread is part of a garment, a significant length is two fingers. This is the amount of Tzitzith string that must be "on the corner." If the hole is placed any closer than this, the significant amount will not be "on the corner" but "beneath the corner."[52]

We also have a rule that a piece of cloth that is more than three fingers square must be taken into account. If the hole through which the Tzitzith are attached was more than three fingers from the edge, it would be separated from it by a significant piece of the garment. It would then no longer be "on the corner," but inside the main body of the garment. For this reason the hole of the Tzitzith must be no more than three fingers from the edge of the garment.[53]

We therefore see that the hole through which the Tzitzith are attached must lie between two and three fingers from the edge of the Tallith. If we wish to take into account all opinions regarding the length of a "finger," we would have to place it between 2 and 2¼ inches from the edge.[54] If it is at least 1½ inches from

[51] *Menachoth* 42a, *Yad, Tzitzith* 1:6, *Orach Chaim* 11:9. This is approximately two fingers, cf. *Beth Yosef, Orach Chaim* 11 (16a) s.v. *VaYaaseh,* quoting Mahari Ibn Chabib; *Rav Shulchan Arukh* 11:16.

[52] *Sefer Mitzvoth Gadol (Smag),* positive commandment 26; *Beth Yosef, loc. cit.; Orach Chaim* 11:9.

[53] *Menachoth* 42a; *Beth Yosef loc. cit.*

[54] According to the opinion that a finger is one inch, it must be at least two inches from the edge. But according to those who maintain that a finger is ¾ inch, since it can be no more than 3 fingers, the maximum distance it may be from the edge is 2¼ inches.

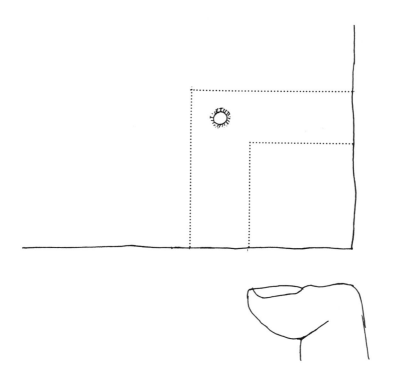

the edge, however, the Tallith may be worn. (See figure 2)

Conclusion

From all this, we clearly see that the Tzitzith are much more than mere "strings." There is a richness of law and lore surrounding them that bespeaks a most profound depth. Furthermore, their structure in *Halakhah* (Jewish Religious Law) involves some of the deepest discussions in the entire Talmud.

One point bears repeating. The strings used for Tzitzith must be spun especially for this purpose. Therefore, when one buys a Tallith, *Tallith Katan*, or Tzitzith to be put into a Tallith, it is most important that one make certain that the Tzitzith were made in the proper manner. This is especially true in the case of silk, rayon and nylon Tzitzith, where extreme caution must be exercised.

There are two ways in which we observe the commandment of Tzitzith. One is through the *Tallith Katan*—the "small Tallith"—which we wear as part of our clothing. The second is the *Tallith Gadol*—the "great Tallith"—worn in the synagogue.

Of the two, the Tallith worn in the synagogue is by far the most familiar. In many ways, however, the *Tallith Katan*, which is worn all day, is more important. We will therefore begin our discussion with the *Tallith Katan*.

THE TALLITH KATAN

In proclaiming the commandment of Tzitzith, the Torah says, "You shall make tassels (*Gedilim*) on the *four corners* of your garments. . . ." From this we learn that Tzitzith are only required on a four-cornered garment.[55]

In ancient times, many garments were four-cornered.[56] Clothing was not tailored as it is today, but most often consisted of a simple rectangle of cloth, direct from the loom, which was worn as a shawl, cape, tunic or toga. As late as the classical Greek period, the standard garments consisted of the *chiton* and *himation*, which were essentially rectangles of cloth, draped and fastened around the body. Similar garments were worn in Talmudic times. Since everyone wore four-cornered clothing, they fulfilled the commandment of Tzitzith merely by placing them on their regular garb.

Because we no longer regularly wear four-cornered

---

[55] See note 24.

[56] *Tosafoth, Arkhin* 2b, s.v. *HaKol, Tosafoth Yeshenim, Shabbath* 32b s.v. *BeAvon*, Abarbanel on Numbers 15:38.

clothing, we wear a special garment in order to fulfill this most important commandment.[57] One of the most important Jewish commentators, Rabbi Yitzchak Abarbanel, stated that this is the reason why the Torah states that we must "make Tzitzith . . . for all generations." Even though a time would come when four-cornered garments would not normally be worn, we must continue to wear a special garment in order to fulfill the commandment of Tzitzith.[58]

This special garment is the *Tallith Katan*—the "small Tallith." It is also sometimes called an *Arba Kanfoth*—literally "four corners"—or simply "Tzitzith." In Yiddish it was often referred to as a *Lahbsideckel*, or "body cover."

The *Tallith Katan* consists of a simple rectangle of cloth, with a hole for the neck. Two styles are shown in figure 3.

The *Tallith Katan* should be at least a cubit (or *Amah*) square on each side. According to our discussion on measurements, this would be between 18 and 24 inches. If possible, it is best to wear the larger size, and thus be covered according to even the stricter opinion.

You should wear the *Tallith Katan* all day long. It is worn under your shirt, preferably over an undershirt, and is put on the first thing in the morning.

If you do not wear a Tallith in synagogue, you should say the following blessing before putting on the *Tallith Katan*:[59]

---

[57] *Menachoth* 41a, *Tosafoth Pesachim* 113b s.v. *VeAin, Tosafoth Yeshenim loc. cit.; Rokeach* 361 (p. 247); *Orach Chaim* 24:1.

[58] Abarbanel, *loc. cit.*

[59] *Nimukey Yosef, Hilkhoth Tzitzith* (Rif 12a) s.v. *Amar, Kol Bo* 22; *Orach Chaim* 8:6 in *Hagah*.

בָּרוּךְ אַתָּה יְיָ אֱלֹהֵינוּ מֶלֶךְ הָעוֹלָם, אֲשֶׁר
קִדְּשָׁנוּ בְּמִצְוֹתָיו וְצִוָּנוּ עַל מִצְוַת צִיצִית.

Barukh Atah Adonoy Elohenu Melekh ha-olam asher kid'sha-nu be-mitzvo-thav ve-tziva-nu al Mitzvath Tzitzith.

Blessed are You God, our Lord, King of the world, who has made us holy with His commandments and gave us the Mitzvah of Tzitzith.

If you put on the *Tallith Katan* before washing your hands, you can defer the blessing until later, taking hold of the Tzitzith when you recite it.[60]

If you normally wear a Tallith, according to most authorities, it is best not to say the blessing over the *Tallith Katan* at all. Instead, you should have in mind to include it when you say the blessing over the Tallith.[61]

The *Tallith Katan* should be worn all day long. Some people also wear it to sleep.[62]

It is also a custom for some people to keep their Tzitzith exposed, in order that they constantly fulfill the injunction, "and you shall see them."[63] This, however, is not a strict requirement, and the Tzitzith may be worn completely under one's clothing.[64]

---

[60] *Tosafoth, Menachoth* 36a s.v. *U'KeSheHigia, Berachoth* 14b s.v. *U'Manach, Orach Chaim* 8:10.

[61] *Darkey Moshe, Orach Chaim* 8:3, *Aruch HaShulchan* 8:16, *Mishneh Berurah* 8:24; *Darkey Chaim VeShalom* 32.

[62] *Darkey Chaim VeShalom* 38.

[63] *Orach Chaim* 8:11; *Magen Avraham* 8:13; *Mishneh Berurah* 8:26.

[64] *T'shuvoth Mahari Bruno* 96.

Since the *Tallith Katan* is always worn, the Mitzvah of Tzitzith is one Mitzvah that is observed most constantly. It is the first commandment that we observe in the morning,[65] and continues throughout the day. As such, it is a constant reminder of our obligation as Jews, and of our allegiance to God.

Through the *Tallith Katan*, the Mitzvah of Tzitzith is one of the very first observances that we teach a child. In many communities, it is a custom to present a child with his first *Tallith Katan* on his third birthday; from then on, it is constantly worn.[66]

The *Tallith Katan* is also one of the least expensive ritual objects that you can purchase. Its cost is negligible, and yet, its spiritual benefits can be priceless.

---

[65] *Likutey Halachoth, Tzitzith* 3:1 (35b), *Netilath Yadayim* 4:8.
[66] *Sukkah* 42a; *Arakhin* 2b; *Tosefta Chagiga* 1:3, *Orach Chaim* 17:3; *Shaarey T'shuvah* 17:2; *Likutey Halachoth loc. cit.*

THE TALLITH

The second, and more familiar manner in which we fulfill the commandment of Tzitzith is through the Tallith, which is worn primarily during the morning prayer services.[67] The fact that we pray in a Tallith is alluded to in the verse, "The prayer of a poor man, when he enwraps himself [in a Tallith] and pours out his words before God" (*Psalms 102:1*). When we stand before God like beggars, in prayer and supplication, we are to wrap ourselves in a Tallith.[68]

There are a number of diverse customs regarding the Tallith. In some communities, young men do not begin wearing a Tallith until they are married.[69] In others, the

---

[67] *Tosafoth, Berachoth* 14b s.v. *U'Meniach; Yad, Tzitzith* 3:11; *Orach Chaim* 24:1. *Cf. Midrash Tehillim* 35:2; Ibn Ezra on Numbers 15:39; Bachya *ibid.; Smag, positive* 26; *Zohar* 3:226b; *Shaar HaKavanoth, Tzitzith* 1 (p. 24).

[68] *Zohar* 3:278a; *Tikuney Zohar* 11 (26b), 21 (55b). *Cf. Metzudoth Tzion ad loc.*

[69] *Tashbatz* 462; Maharil, *Hilchoth Nisuin* (Jerusalem, 5729) p. 65a; quoted in *Be'er Hetiv, Orach Chaim* 17:4; *Darkey Chaim VeShalom* 37. See note

Tallith is worn immediately after Bar Mitzvah. In all such cases, one follows the custom of his congregation. An important point must, however, be made. In congregations where many teenagers do not wear the *Tallith Katan*, they *must* wear a Tallith for the morning service. It is most important that Tzitzith be worn during this service.

A Tallith should be large enough so that one can drape it over his shoulders, with two corners in front and the other two in back.[70] A good Tallith should therefore measure at least four feet by six feet and be large enough to cover the individual down to his waist. As an absoulte minimum, it must measure one cubit or *Amah* (24 inches) in width.

Although a Tallith can be made of any type of cloth, it is preferable to make it of pure white wool.[71] Whenever the Torah speaks of a garment, the reference is usually to either a woolen or linen garment.[72] (Now that we do not have the blue wool to place in the Tzitzith, a linen Tallith is not used.[73]) Therefore, when one wears a woolen Tallith, he is performing the Mitzvah exactly as it was done in Biblical times, and such a Tallith is considered a "garment" in the fullest sense of Torah usage. Besides, wearing a woolen Tallith has become the hallmark of the individual who is sophisticated and observant in the best possible Jewish sense.

[70] *Orach Chaim* 8:4, 10:12; *Turey Zahav* 10:9; *Mishneh Berurah* 10:37. *Cf. Midrash Abkir* on Exodus 14:29; *Midrash Tehillim* 6:1; *Yalkut* 2:723; *Tosafoth, Arakhin* 2b s.v. *HaYodea, Hagahoth Maimonioth Tzitzith* 3:9 #20.
[71] *Turey Zahav* 9:8; *Mishneh Berurah* 9:16. *Cf. Shabbath* 153a; *Bach, Orach Chaim* 24 s.v. *BeKol;* Rashi, *Menachoth* 38b s.v. *Midey.*
[72] *Shabbath* 26b; *Yebamoth* 4b; *Menachoth* 39b.
[73] *Tur Orach Chaim* 9 (12a); *Orach Chaim* 9:6. *Cf. Tosafoth, Menachoth* 40a s.v. *Sadin.*

On weekdays, when Tefillin are worn, the Tallith is put on first.[74] There is a general rule that the Mitzvah performed most often takes precedence. Judaism is more a religion of steadfastness than one of dramatic highlights. Therefore, since the Tallith is also worn on the Sabbath and holidays, while the Tefillin are not, the Tallith takes precedence.[75]

Before putting on the Tallith, you should check the Tzitzith and make sure that they have not become torn. If they are tangled, you should separate them, so that they hang down like "loose hairs."[76] In many places, it is a custom to place the folded Tallith on one's shoulder while doing this.

Just before you put on the Tallith, you should say, "I am now about to fulfill God's commandment to wear Tzitzith on my garment, in order that I remember and observe all His commandments." There is also a longer declaration found in most prayer books.

The Tallith is put on while standing. You should hold the Tallith over your head and say the blessing:

בָּרוּךְ אַתָּה יְיָ אֱלֹהֵינוּ מֶלֶךְ הָעוֹלָם, אֲשֶׁר קִדְּשָׁנוּ בְּמִצְוֹתָיו וְצִוָּנוּ לְהִתְעַטֵּף בַּצִּיצִית.

Baruch Atah Adonoy Elohenu Melekh ha-olam asher kid'sha-nu be-mitzvo-thav ve-tziva-nu le-hithatef ba-Tzitzith.

Blessed are You God, our Lord, King of

[74] *Orach Chaim* 25:1.
[75] *Berachoth* 51b; *Pesachim* 114a; *Sukkah* 54b, *Megillah* 29b; *Beth Yosef, Orach Chaim* 25 s.v. *VeAchar; Turey Zahav* 25:1.
[76] *Menachoth* 42a, *Orach Chaim* 8:7.

the world, who made us holy with His commandments and bid us to enwrap ourselves in
Tzitzith.

You should then drape the Tallith over your head,
and cast the corners over your left shoulder. This is
what the Talmud means when it states that one should
enwrap himself with a Tallith, "as the Arabs (Ishmael-
ites) enwrap themselves."[77] There are a number of customs regarding this.

You should stand wrapped in this Tallith in this manner long enough to walk four cubits, or approximately
four seconds. While enwrapped in the Tallith, it is customary to say (*Psalm 36:8,11*):[78]

מַה יָּקָר חַסְדְּךָ אֱלֹהִים, וּבְנֵי אָדָם בְּצֵל כְּנָפֶיךָ יֶחֱסָיוּן: יִרְוְיֻן
מִדֶּשֶׁן וְנַחַל עֲדָנֶיךָ תַשְׁקֵם: כִּי עִמְּךָ מְקוֹר חַיִּים, בְּאוֹרְךָ
נִרְאֶה אוֹר: מְשֹׁךְ חַסְדְּךָ לְיֹדְעֶיךָ וְצִדְקָתְךָ לְיִשְׁרֵי לֵב:

How precious is Your love, O God,
    man finds shelter
    in the shadow cast
    by the corners of Your [Tallith].
They feast on the riches of Your house,
    You let them drink Your rivers of
    delight.

---

[77] *Magen Avraham* 9:2; *Rav Shulchan Arukh* 8:5; *Ba'er Hetiv* 8:3; *Mish-neh Berurah* 8:4. Cf. *Tosafoth, Arakhin* 2b *HaYodea*, from *Moed Katan* 24a; *Rokeach* 361 (p. 248); *Shaar HaKavanoth, Tzitzith* 2 (p. 32), *Pri Etz Chaim, Tzitzith* 1 (p. 65). See also *Ben Ish Chay (Halachoth) Bereshith* 5, *T'shuvoth Lechem Shlomo* 13, *Darkey Chaim VeShalom* 34.

[78] *Pri Etz Chaim, Tzitzith* 6, note 1 (p. 81).

[79] See note 70.

For the source of life is with You,
    by Your light, we see light.
Bring Your love to those who know You,
    Your charity to upright hearts.

Since this is said while your head is covered with the Tallith, you will have to learn it by heart.

You should then rearrange the Tallith so that two Tzitzith are in front, and two in back. You are thus surrounded by the Tzitzith.

In many communities, it is customary for married men to cover their heads with the Tallith. Unmarried boys, however, even where they do wear a Tallith, never cover their heads with it.[80]

It is also a very ancient practice for the one leading the service (the *Shliach Tzibur* or *Chazzan*) to wear a Tallith. As we shall see, there is a most profound significance underlying this custom.

In order to beautify the Mitzvah, many observant Jews place a border or *Atarah* of pure silver on the Tallith. This is done to make the observance as beautiful and meaningful as possible.

Now that you know something of the Halakhic structure of Tzitzith and how to put them on, you might like to make a pair yourself.

---

[80] *Magen Avraham* 8:3. *Cf.* Rashi, *Kiddushin* 29b s.v. *DeLo; Beth Yosef, Orach Chaim* 8 (9a) *U'Mechase.*

MAKE YOUR OWN

There is nothing very mysterious about making a Tallith, or *Tallith Katan*. Each one is simply a rectangle of cloth. Tzitzith are a bit more involved, but are so easy to put in that even a young child can do it.

To make a Tallith, all you need is a good piece of pure white woolen cloth. It should be 4 feet by 6 feet in size.

For a *Tallith Katan*, you can use any sort of cloth, although wool is still best. It should measure at least 18 by 36 inches, and preferably 24 by 48. Cut a T-shaped hole for the neck.

For both a Tallith and *Tallith Katan*, you then make a hole approximately two inches from each edge (measured perpendicularly, not diagonally). Through this hole the Tzitzith are placed.

It is a good idea to hem both the Tallith and the hole, so that they will not tear. When doing so, you must use a thread made of a different material than the Tallith.[81] For example, if you are making a Tallith out of wool,

[81] *Orach Chaim* 15:6.

you should sew the hem with cotton or silk. If you are making a cotton *Tallith Katan*, sew the hem with silk or rayon thread (but not wool). In no case, however, should you use linen thread, since together with the woolen Tzitzith, this would constitute *Shaatnez*.

You are now ready to place the Tzitzith in the Tallith or *Tallith Katan*.

Making Tzitzith

Whether or not you make your own, there are occasions when you may want to put Tzitzith on a Tallith or *Tallith Katan*. You might buy a Tallith and desire to put in your own Tzitzith or replace the ones already in. The Tzitzith may have become worn or torn and might need replacement. In any case, it is useful to know how to make them.

You can buy Tzitzith from any good Jewish book store, or your rabbi or advisor can order you a set. Look for rabbinical certification stating that they are made of thread spun especially for Tzitzith. Your rabbi can serve as your guide in this area.

The package of Tzitzith will contain 16 strings, four for each corner. Four of these strings will be longer than the rest, and they are usually wound around the others. One of these longer strings is used in each corner as the *Shamash* or "servant" string; this is the one you will use to make the windings.

Separate the strings and you are ready to begin:

1. Take all four strings and place them through the hole. Adjust them so that they are all even (except for the *Shamash*, which remains longer on one

side). The four strings are now doubled into eight.

2. Make a double knot, with four strings on each side. (It does not matter whether you make a square knot or a granny knot.) Before making the first knot, you should say, "I am doing this to fulfill the commandment of Tzitzith," or *LeShem Mitzvath Tzitzith* in Hebrew.
3. Take the *Shamash* and wind it around the other seven strings. Make seven windings.
4. Make another double knot.
5. Eight windings.
6. A double knot.
7. Eleven windings.
8. A double knot.
9. Thirteen windings.
10. A final double knot.

Your Tzitzith are now complete. It's as easy as that! Your Tzitzith should contain five knots and four groups of windings. The total number of windings should be 39.

Now that we have explored some of the basics of Tzitzith, we can look into their deeper significance.

A DEEPER LOOK

"Open my eyes, that I may behold the wonders of Your Torah."

(Psalms 119:18)

CLOTHING

One of the most obvious points about Tzitzith is the fact that they involve a commandment directly related to clothing. They are not a Mitzvah in their own right as are Tefillin, but one that pertains to the garments we wear. If we are to understand fully the meaning of Tzitzith, we must first explore the significance that clothing plays in human society.

Of all living creatures, man is unique in the fact that he covers his body with clothing. *Homo Sapiens* is the only species that wears clothing. The reason for this has been the subject of study for philosophers, sociologists, anthropologists, psychologists and ethnologists for many years, and they have come up with some interesting theories. Even more fascinating is the fact that their conclusions often agree with those taught by our great religious sages.

The most obvious reason for wearing clothing might appear to be to provide protection from the elements. However, when anthropologists studied primitive tribes in even the warmest climates, they found that people still wore clothing as a matter of course. The human practice of wearing clothing seems to be universal, even where there is no need for protection from the elements.[1]

What was discovered was that people covered their sexual organs in virtually every human society. Let us now see how this agrees with the Torah view.

One of the most intriguing stories in the Torah is that of Adam's sin. We all know the story: How the serpent tempted Eve to eat of the Tree of Knowledge (*Etz HaDaath*), and, as a result, both Adam and Eve were cursed and driven out of the Garden of Eden. Taken superficially, this is an intriguing story; but on a deeper level, it provides us with a profound insight into human psychology.

The existence of a walking, talking serpent might seem difficult to understand, but our sages teach us that it was the very incarnation of evil. In order for man to have free will, at least the possibility of evil had to exist.[2] Before Adam sinned, evil was not part of man, but something external. It was therefore represented by the serpent, an entity external to man. It was only after man sinned that evil became an integral part of his being.[3] From then on, man's battle with evil became as much a battle with himself as one against an external force.

Before Adam sinned, the Torah says of him, "And they were both naked, the man and his wife, and they were not ashamed" (*Genesis 2:25*). Our sages comment that they were not ashamed because they had no sexual desire.[4] Sex was as natural a body function as eating

---

[1] Cf. Abarbanel on Genesis 3:7.

[2] See below, note 28.

[3] *Nefesh HaChaim* 1:6, note s.v. *VeHaInyan* (6a).

[4] *Cf.* Rashi, Sforno, Abarbanel *ad loc.*; Ramban on Genesis 2:9. See notes 6 and 11.

and drinking. It was something completely under man's control. Sexual pleasure may have been something that they could enjoy, but it was not the overwhelming passion that it is today, where it drives people to foolish and even destructive acts. Sex, like the serpent, was something external to man. Man could enjoy it when he wanted to, but he was not driven by it.

Since sexual desire was not an integral part of man's nature, there was no shame in exposing the sexual organs. They were no different than his eyes, ears, hands or feet. They were not something that could arouse another individual, or in any way make one feel like a sex object.[5] Indeed, so innocent and natural was the sexual act, that Adam and Eve did not even feel compelled to perform it in private.[6]

The external incarnation that led them to sin was represented by the serpent. It is a well known fact that in almost every culture the serpent represents some sort of phallic symbol. To a large degree then, the serpent represents sexual temptation. Our sages teach us that the main temptation the serpent used to lure Eve was that of sex.[7]

As soon as man sinned, he began to have an Evil Urge or *Yetzer HaRa*. Evil was no longer something outside of himself, but an integral part of his being. It was now a force that man could overcome only with the greatest difficulty.

Our sages teach us that, "The Evil Urge exists mainly

[5] *Cf.* Alshech on Genesis 2:25.

[6] *Ibid. Cf. Bereshith Rabbah* 18:6; Maharazav *ad loc.; Idem.* 85:2.

[7] *Shabbath* 146a, Rashi *ad loc.* s.v. *KeSheBa, Yebamos* 103b; *Avodah Zarah* 22b; *Bechoroth* 8a; *Tosefta Sotah* 4:5; *Akedath Yitzchak* 9 (73b).

in the area of sex."[8] Very often, it is sexual temptation that leads a person away from religion and godliness in other areas. It is often the strongest barrier standing in the way of an individual's spiritual perfection.

On the other hand, the individual who can completely control his sexual desires is counted as one who can control all his emotions. Here again, our sages teach us that a person is only called a Tzadik or saint when he can control his sexual passions.[9] The main path to holiness is through self-mastery, and the most difficult area for such mastery is sex. To achieve such self-mastery takes great internal strength, to which our sages allude when they say, "Who is strong? He who overcomes his passions."[10]

As soon as man sinned, his sexuality was aroused. Immediately after Adam and Eve ate of the Fruit of Knowledge, the Torah tells us, "The eyes of both of them were opened, and they knew that they were naked. They sewed fig leaves and made themselves loincloths" (Genesis 3:7). The major commentators explain that now that their sexual desires were aroused, they were ashamed to stand naked. They had begun to view others as sex objects, and were themselves ashamed to be seen in that light.[11]

It is interesting to note how closely the opinions of social scientists parallel the Torah. Where science seeks with an unprejudiced eye, it is merely another way of

---

[8] Zohar 3:15b. Cf. Rashi, Megillah 31a s.v. Korin; Turey Zahav, Orach Chaim 622:4.

[9] Zohar 159b, Nitzutzey Or ad loc. 5 and 6.

[10] Avoth 5:1.

[11] Sforno, Or HaChaim, Abarbanel, Alshech ad loc.; Moreh Nebukhim 1:2; Rashi on Genesis 3:11; Tikuney Zohar 58; Reshith Chochmah, Shaar HaKedushah 16 (196b); Likutey Halachoth, Netilath Yadayim 4:12; Ben Ish Chay, introduction to Bereshith.

approaching truth. In this particular area, honest investigation had discovered a truth revealed in the Torah thousands of years ago.

Even more interesting is the fact that some of these concepts are indicated by the very etymology of the Hebrew language. Hebrew is called the "Holy Tongue" (*Lashon HaKodesh*), and as such, even its grammatical and etymological rules teach us important lessons. In the area under discussion, we see an important case in point.

First of all, the Hebrew word for "garment" is *Le-BHUSH* (לְבוּשׁ) (The capitalized letters indicate those actually used in the Hebrew spelling.) This comes from the word *BUSH* (בּוּשׁ), which means "to be ashamed."[12] The very structure of the Hebrew language indicates that clothing is worn because of shame.

Another Hebrew word for garment is *BeGeD* (בֶּגֶד). This has the same root as the word *BaGaD* (בָּגַד), meaning "to rebel."[13] This indicates that man wears clothing because he originally rebelled against God. Before man sinned and rebelled, he was perfectly content and unashamed of being nude.

God also understood that in his fallen state man had a need for clothing. The Torah states that before ejecting man from the Garden of Eden, "God made garments of skins for Adam and his wife, and He clothed them" (*Genesis 3:21*).

From all this, we see that the main function of human clothing is to act as barrier against sexual desires. As

---

[12] Abarbanel on Genesis 2:25. *Cf. Shabbath* 77b.

[13] *Zohar* 3:175a, 3:276a. *Cf. Sahnedrin* 37a, *Yerushalmi Peah* 1:1 (5a); *BeMidbar Rabbah* 10:1; *Agudath Bereshith* 42; *Reshith Chochmah, Shaar HaKedusha* 6 (142c); *Degel Machaneh Ephraim, Sh'lach* (58b); *Likutey Halachoth, Tzitzith* 5:10 (45b).

such, it is particularly related to the sense of sight. The purpose of clothing is to cover the body in order that it not be visible as a source of sexual arousal.

We can now understand the purpose of Tzitzith.

Here again, we can actually see this in the etymological structure of the word. The word *TziTzith* (צִיצִית) has the same root as the word *TzuTz*, (צוּץ), meaning "to look."[14] Tzitzith are therefore something that relate specifically to the sense of sight, something to look at.

The Torah says of the Tzitzith, "You shall *see* them, and not stray after your heart and after *your eyes*, which have led you to immorality." The Talmud explains that the injunction not to stray "after your eyes" refers to visual sexual stimulation.[15] Clothing in general acts as a natural barrier to such arousal, and the Tzitzith serve to reinforce this barrier.

None of this, however, is meant to imply that sex is something dirty or evil. To the contrary, Judaism looks upon sex as something beautiful and pleasurable. The Torah views sexual relations between husband and wife as something normal, desirable, and the one act that does the most to strengthen the bond of love between them.[16] But at the same time, the Torah realizes that when misused, sex can be a most destructive and debilitating force. Historians tell us of entire civilizations that have fallen as a result of sexual corruption, and here again, this view is reflected in our Torah's teachings.[17]

---

[14] *Sifri* (115), Rashi, Rashbam, on Numbers 15:38, *Zohar* 3:174b, *Akedath Yitzchak* 77 (4:43b). See *Bahir* 92, that the 32 strings of the Tzitzith are called watchers. Cf. *Maaloth HaSulam* on *Zohar* 3:301a.

[15] *Berachoth* 13a.

[16] Cf. Exodus 21:10, Rashi *ad loc.*; *Niddah* 31b.

[17] Cf. *Yerushalmi Sotah* 1:5 (6a); *Bereshith Rabbah* 26:10; *VaYikra Rabbah* 23:9; *Tanchuma Bereshith* 12; Rashi on Genesis 6:13.

The type of sex that the Torah proscribes is that which is irresponsible, exploitative and destructive. The commandment of Tzitzith was given as a safeguard against such activity.

In the Talmud, we find a most interesting story that illustrates this:[18]

There was a man who was most careful to observe the Mitzvah of Tzitzith. Once he heard that there was a harlot in a port city who charged 400 gold pieces for her services. He sent her the 400 gold pieces and arranged a rendezvous.

When the appointed time came, he traveled to her city, and waited outside her door. Her attendant informed her that the man who had sent 400 gold pieces had arrived and was waiting outside. The harlot replied, "Let him enter."

She arranged seven beds, six of silver, and the seventh of gold. Next to the beds, she placed seven ladders, six of silver, and the uppermost of gold. Finally, she disrobed and sat herself on the highest bed.

The man was beginning to undress when suddenly his four Tzitzith began to slap him in his face. He slipped down and sat on the ground.

The woman joined him and also sat on the ground. She exclaimed, "By Jupiter! I will not let you leave me until you tell me what you find wrong with me."

The man replied, "I [swear] by the Divine Service that I have never seen a woman as beautiful as you! But our God has given us a commandment known as Tzitzith. [In the section dealing with the commandment,] it is written, 'I am Hashem your God,' two times. 'I am' the One who will eventually reward—and 'I am' the One who will eventually punish. [The Tzitzith]

[18] *Menachoth* 44a, *Sifri* (115) on Numbers 15:41.

appeared to me like four witnesses [who would testify against me for my sin]."

The woman said, "I [swear] by the Divine Service that I will not let you leave me until you tell me your name, your city, your rabbi, and the school where you studied Torah."

He wrote the information on a paper and left. The woman then sold all her possessions, giving a third of the proceeds to the government (to allow her to leave), a third to the poor, and keeping a third for herself. The only other thing that she kept was her beds.

She then went to Rabbi Chiya's academy and said, "Rabbi, teach me and allow me to convert to Judaism."

The Rabbi demurred, saying, "My daughter, is it because you have set your eyes on one of my students?"

She then showed him the note [and related the entire story.] The Rabbi finally [agreed to convert her and] said, "Go, my daughter, and take what is yours. The same beds that you used for sin, you may now enjoy in a permissible manner."

The great commentator, Rabbi Moshe Alshech (1521–1593) explains that the Tzitzith did not actually slap him in the face physically.[19] Rather, they struck at him psychologically, as he later recounted, so that they suddenly seemed like four witnesses, ready to testify against him.

This account, however, shows dramatically how Tzitzith can help one master his sexual compulsions.

The passage of Tzitzith tells us to "look at them and remember all of God's commandments, and not stray after your heart and eyes." Sexual desire is the one

---

[19] Alshech on Numbers 15:41 (31d). Cf. Iyun Yaakov (in Eyn Yaakov) ad loc.

thing that is most often responsible for leading a person away from religious observance. Sex is most readily available among those who are indifferent or antagonistic toward religion. In seeking to court the favor of those who will provide him with sexual outlets, one may be sorely tempted to give up such things as the Sabbath, Kashruth, and other important elements of Judaism. One who is drawn into a society of sexual promiscuity finds himself in an environment hostile to true Jewish values. This is not mere theory. There are countless cases of religious individuals who have left the ranks of religious observance in order to pursue their sexual infatuations.

The Talmud tells us that when the Torah says, "You shall not stray after your heart," the reference is to atheism.[20] This is also borne out by experience. There is nothing that will draw a person away from God more than sexual promiscuity. Many indeed are the Jewish youth who have given up God completely in order to gain some fleeting sexual pleasure. All too many are those who have sacrificed all the depth and meaning that they have gained from Judaism for the dubious promise of sexual "freedom." And looming above this is the danger of intermarriage, which leads a tragic number of our youth away from Judaism completely.

If we look in the Torah, we find an important example of this. Soon after the Jews came near the borders of ancient Moab, the Torah relates, "Israel remained in Shittim, and the people began to behave promiscuously with the daughters of Moab. They invited the people to sacrifice to their gods, and the people came and ate and bowed down to their gods" (*Numbers* 20:1,2). This is

[20] *Berachoth* 13a.

one of the first recorded cases where sexual infatuation led many Jews to abandon the teachings of the Torah. Things have not changed very much since then.

The verse dealing with Tzitzith then says, "In order that you remember and keep all My commandments, and be holy to your God." Here again, the Torah is telling us that the main path to holiness is mastery of one's sexuality.[21] In protecting the individual from promiscuity, Tzitzith can lead him to holiness.

The verse ends with a reference to the Exodus. The Exodus represents both a physical and spiritual liberation, but in an important sense, it also involves the liberation from domination by one's sexual appetites. When the Torah speaks of forbidden sexual activity, it introduces the section with the statement, "You shall no longer do what was done in the land of Egypt where you dwelt" (Leviticus 18:3). Egypt was known as a place of extreme sexual immorality. When the Jews left Egypt, this was one of the things that they were to leave behind.[22] In serving to check our passions, the Tzitzith tend to reinforce this aspect of the Exodus.

The Tzitzith may seem like simple strings, but they can affect an individual's entire lifestyle. It is now useful to look even more deeply into their true significance.

---

[21] Rashi on Leviticus 19:2; VaYikra Rabbah 24:6.
[22] Sifri, Rashi ad loc.

GOD'S TALLITH

Rabbi Yochanan said: If it were not written [in the Bible] it would be impossible to say. But we are taught that God wrapped Himself [in a Tallith] like a prayer leader and showed Moses the order of prayer. He said, "Whenever Israel sins, let them proceed in this manner, and I will forgive them."

Talmud, Rosh HaShanah 17b

In this short lesson, Rabbi Yochanan is presenting us with a most remarkable teaching. According to most commentators, the Biblical verse to which he is referring is, 'The Ancient of Days (*Atik Yomin*) sat there, His garment was white as snow, and the hair of His head was like pure wool" (*Daniel 7:9*).[23] It is also closely related to the verse, "He covers Himself with light as a garment" (*Psalms 104:2*).[24]

This is a very difficult lesson to understand. How can we say that God performs a physical act like putting on a Tallith? We know that it is a fundamental principle of

---

[23] *Mesorath HaShas ad loc. Cf. Zohar 3:140b, Derekh Mitzvothekha (Chabad) Tzitzith (15b); Likutey Halachoth, Tzitzith 2:2; Bach, Orach Chaim 24 s.v. BeKol.*

[24] Maharsha *ad loc. Cf. Zohar 1:13b; Tikuney Zohar 21 (55b). Also see Bereshith Rabbah 1:6, 3:4; Sh'moth Rabbah 50:1; Devarim Rabbah 2:37; Tanchuma VaYak'hel 6.*

Judaism to realize that God has no body, shape or form.[25] God is in no way physical, and nothing physical can apply to Him at all. To suggest anything physical such as a body or a Tallith with relation to God would go against the very foundations of our belief.

Still, in the Torah and in many other places, we see that God is spoken of as if He had a human body. In countless verses, we find expression such as "the hand of God" or "the eyes of God." Numerous other parts of the body are also mentioned with relation to God. All such references are called *anthropomorphisms*— expressions where we borrow terms from human experience when speaking of God.

Obviously, all such expressions must be understood allegorically rather than literally. Our sages teach us that God borrows terms from His creatures to express His relationship to the world.[26] A physical allegory may be used to express a very profound philosophical relationship between God and His creation. Thus, for example, when the Torah speaks of "God's hand," it is speaking of His expression of power and of His providence in guiding the world's destiny. Similarly, when it speaks of "God's eyes," it is alluding to the fact that He is aware of everything that happens in the world. The same is true of all other such anthropomorphisms.

Anthropomorphisms such as "hand" and "eye" are fairly simple to understand. But when we try to understand the full richness of such allegories in our sacred literature, we find ourselves in a much more difficult situation. One of the greatest Jewish thinkers, the Ram-

---

[25] Thirteen Principles #3.
[26] *Mechilta* (65a); Rashi, on Exodus 19:18; *Tanchuma Yithro* 13; *Bereshith Rabbah* 27:1; *Koheleth Rabbah* 2:24; *Yad, Yesodey HaTorah* 1:9.

bam (Maimonides), states that a full interpretation of these would involve some of the deepest mysteries of Judaism.[27] This is an area where many of our greatest sages over the centuries have delved, explaining and expounding these deep concepts.

It is obvious that when our sages teach us that God wears a Tallith, they are providing us with a profound lesson concerning God's relationship to us. In speaking of Tzitzith, the Torah says that the reason for this commandment is so that "you should remember all of God's commandments." Obviously, then, this lesson also has something to do with the significance of the commandments. Let us try to understand it more completely.

The Problem of Evil

One of the questions that philosophers and thinkers have puzzled over for centuries is the problem of evil. If God is all good, why does He allow evil to exist? Why is it possible for people to harm each other? Why are such things as wars and concentration camps possible in a world created and ruled by God?

This is a question that is adequately treated by our great sages and teachers. But before we can begin to delve into their explanations, we must first try to answer an even more basic question:

Why did God create the world?

Obviously, it would be utterly naive to believe that we could ever fully answer this question. God is so high above us that we can no more understand His motives than a fly can understand the work of a great mathematician around whom it buzzes. God is so high that we

---

[27] Rambam on *Sanhedrin* 10:1, Seventh Principle.

cannot even begin to comprehend His purpose.

Yet, we can understand God's reasons to the extent that they have been revealed by Him in the Torah. The account of creation ends with the words, "God saw everything that He had made, and it was very good" (*Genesis 1:31*). This and similar passages teach us that God's purpose in creation was to do good. In order to express His love and goodness, God had to create a world. This essentially is what the Pslamist means when he sings, "God is good to all, His love rests over all His works" (*Psalms 145:9*).

But since God is infinitely and ultimately good, it would stand to reason that if He wanted to give good to His creation, it would have to be the highest possible good. What is that? What is the highest ultimate good?

The answer should be perfectly obvious. This ultimate good is God Himself. God thus created a world to which He could give of Himself.

But how is this possible? In what way can God give of Himself? How can a mere man partake of God?

The answer is not difficult if you really think about it. We can partake of God by resembling Him to the greatest possible degree. The more we resemble Him, the more we partake of the ultimate good that is God.

It is for this reason that God gave man free will. If man did not have free will, he would be poles apart from God. He would be little more than a robot or puppet. God, on the other hand, is absolutely free to do as He wills, since there is nothing that can hold Him back. In giving man free will, God gave him the ability to imitate God and thus ultimately partake of Him.

Therefore, just as God chose good as a matter of free will, so can man. But in order for this choice to be real, God had to create the opposite of good. He therefore created the possibility of evil, so that man would be free to choose between good and its opposite. God Himself speaks of this when He tells His prophet, "I form light and create darkness, I make peace and create evil—I am God; I do all these things" (*Isaiah 45:7*).[28]

Although evil does not fulfill God's primary purpose in creation, it does fulfill His purpose in a secondary way. In a sense, it is like the peel of a fruit or the shell of a nut. They are in themselves useless, but they serve the secondary purpose of preserving the fruit until it is used. The same is true of evil. It does not serve God's primary purpose of bestowing good, but it does fulfill the secondary purpose of making it possible. Because of this analogy, the forces of evil are often referred to as the "husk" or *Klipah* in relation to God's purpose.[29]

God's ultimate purpose, however, is to do good, and to bring about a world "where all is good."[30] The destiny of evil is to be transformed ultimately into good.[31] Slowly but surely, the world must reach the level of perfection planned by God.

Providence

The major task of perfecting the world belongs to man. The Psalmist said, "The heavens belong to God, but the earth He gave to the sons of man" (*Psalms 115:16*). It is man's responsibility to use his God-given free will for good and thus bring about a world con-

---

[28] In this entire discussion, we follow the outline of *Derech HaShem* 2. For further details, see *God, Man and Tefillin* (NCSY, New York, 1973) p. 35ff.; *The Handbook of Jewish Thought*, Chapter 3.

[29] *Sefer HaYashar* 1.

[30] *Kiddushin* 39b; *Yad, T'shuvah* 9:1.

[31] *KaLaCh Pith'chey Chochmah* #2.

forming to God's plan. In so doing, he becomes a partner with God, and is thus able to partake of Him in yet another sense.

But God does not leave things to chance. There is also an element of Divine Providence. Although God gave individuals free will, He still influences the large scale course of history. Even though He does not determine the conduct of individuals, the collective wills of nations and societies are largely determined by God. This is what scripture means when it says, "The king's heart is in God's hand . . . He turns it however He wills" (*Proverbs 21:1*).[32]

God also guides the destiny of each individual to fulfill His purpose. Man might have free will, but God interacts with him to bring about His goal. He thus might place an individual in a certain predicament, cause him to meet a propitious friend, or otherwise give him opportunities to act in a way that helps lead the world toward God's ultimate goal.[33]

In a way, the situation is very much analogous to the game of a master chess player. Although his opponent has complete free will, the master knows how to counter each move, and thus bring the game to any conclusion he desires. Using this analogy, we can say that God is the ultimate Master, and His game involves all mankind. The stakes are the ultimate triumph of good.

All this comes under the general heading of what we call Divine Providence or *Hashgacha*. It is what we mean when we say that God is "King of the universe."

---

[32] Ralbag, *Metzudoth David, ad loc.; Yad, T'shuvah* 6:5; *Moreh Nebukhim* 2:48; *Berachoth* 55a, Rashi *ad loc.* s.v. *Tzerichim; Emunoth VeDeyoth* end of 4:7 (68a); Radak on Jeremiah 10:23; Maharatz Chayoth on *Megillah* 11a.

[33] *Makkoth* 10a; *Shabbath* 104a.

His providence is constantly at work, guiding the world toward His goal.

Besides this primary providence, however, there must also be secondary elements of providence that God uses specifically to deal with evil. If you think about it, it is obvious that there are two such secondary elements.

First, there is an element of providence that allows evil to exist. Since God's purpose requires the existence of evil, He must, in a sense, hold Himself back from utterly destroying it. Therefore, although God is constantly guiding the world toward good, He still allows evil to exist as long as it serves His purpose. It is of this element of providence that our sages speak when they teach us, "When one comes to defile himself, [God] opens the way for him."[34]

The second element of providence is that which protects from evil. Wherever man comes in contact with evil, God must at least give him the power to be able to overcome it. Furthermore, the power that God gives to evil must not be allowed to become part of His providence and thus make it malignant. It is of this second element of God's providence that our sages speak when they say, "Man's [evil] urge becomes stronger each day, and if God did not help him, he would not be able [to overcome it]."[35]

We therefore see that in order for evil to exist, God must interact with it in two basic ways: First, He must allow it to continue to exist; and second, He must not allow it to overcome the good.

Both of these concepts are alluded to in the beginning

[34] *Yoma* 38b.
[35] *Kiddushin* 30b.

of the prophet Ezekiel's vision. He writes, "I looked, and behold, a stormy wind came out of the north, a great cloud, and a flashing fire. It was surrounded by a glowing light (*Nogah*). From its midst was the likes of the *Chashmal*, from the midst of the fire. And in its midst was the form of four *Chayoth* . . . (*Ezekiel 1:4*).

These verses are among the most mysterious in the Bible, as in this entire vision of Ezekiel. It involves such such deep concepts that our sages proscribed its exposition.[36] We must therefore confine our remarks to the explanations offered by our great commentators and sages. This passage does, however, involve some of our topics under discussion, and we will treat it in that context.

Ezekiel begins this account by saying, "The Heavens were opened, and I saw a vision of God" (*Ezekiel 1:2*). He was looking at an allegory of the very topics that we are discussing. In a sense, he was seeing beyond the mere appearances of this world, and achieving an understanding of God's purpose and providence that underlies it.

The first things that the prophet saw were "a stormy wind . . . a great cloud and a flashing fire." Our sages teach us that these allude to the forces of evil that God allows to exist.[37] These are the forces that separate man from God, and the prophet had to break through them before he could actually see a "vision of God."

The next thing that the prophet saw was a "glowing light," *Nogah* in Hebrew. This alludes to the element of God's providence that sustains evil. It is merely a glim-

---

[36] *Chagigah* 2:1 (11b). See *Moreh Nebukhim*, Introduction to part 3.
[37] *Zohar* 3:227a; *Etz Chaim, Shaar Klipath Nogah* 2 (p. 381). Cf. Rashi, Malbim, *ad loc.*

mer of God's light, like the afterglow that remains in the sky after the sun has set. While pertaining to night and darkness, it still retains a glimmer of daylight. This is often referred to as the "glowing husk," or *Klipath Nogah.*[38]

Then the prophet describes seeing "the likes of the *Chashmal.*" The word *Chashmal* is virtually untranslatable, even though most English translations render it as "electrum" (meaning amber), and in modern Hebrew it is used as the word for electricity. The *Chashmal* actually represents a spiritual force, which is involved in the element of providence that protects from evil. The *Chashmal* thus stands as a barrier between good and evil.[39]

The final thing that the prophet saw were "four *Chayoth.*" The word *Chayoth* literally means "living creatures," and the reference is to a certain type of angel particularly associated with God's providence. It is well to keep the *Chayoth* in mind, since we will return to them in our discussion of Tzitzith.

God's "Garment"

When the Torah uses an anthropomorphism, speaking of God as if He were a man, it is usually making use of a human attribute in its most abstract sense. If we understand what function a certain thing has with rela-

---

[38] *Etz Chaim, Shaar HaChashmal* 2 (p. 293), *Shaar Klipath Nogah* 3 (p. 382), *Shaar Kitzur ABYA* 2 (p. 395). *Cf. Zohar* 3:227a; *Likutey Amarim (Tanya)* 1:1 (6a).

[39] *Etz Chaim, Shaar HaTzelem* 3 (p. 51), *Shaar HaChashmal* 1 (p. 291); *Shaar Kitzur ABYA* 6 (p. 401); *Mavo Shaarim* 6:2:3; *Shaar HaKavanoth, Inyan Levishath Begadim* (pp. 12, 13); *Pri Etz Chaim, Shaar HaTefillah* 3 (p. 19).

tion to man, then, in its most abstract sense, this same function usually applies to God's relationship to the world. Thus, a man works with his hands. Therefore, when we speak of "God's hands," we are referring to His activity. Similarly, man hears with his ears, so when we speak of "God's ears," we are referring to the fact that He hearkens to our prayers. The same is true of all other anthropomorphisms.

If we wish to understand what is meant by God's garment we must go back to our discussion of the function of clothing with respect to man. We can then take this function in its most abstract sense.

As we noted earlier, the main function of human clothing is to serve as a barrier against passion. Much evil would result if man's sexual passions were left unchecked, and in this respect, man's clothing provides protection from this evil.

Taking this in its most abstract sense, we can then say that God's "garment" is also the force that protects from evil.

We can also see this from clothing's secondary function. Man's apparel also serves to protect him from the elements. We can thus say that clothing serves as protection from a hostile environment. The environment hostile to Godliness is, again, evil. In this sense also, we can abstract it to say that God's "garment" is the element of His providence that protects against evil.

This would mean, however, that God's "garment" is identical to the *Chashmal* that we discussed earlier. Both are the elements of His providence that protects from evil. It is therefore not at all surprising that our sages do indeed identify the *Chashmal* with God's "garment," also pointing out that the numerical value or *Gematria* of the word *Chashmal* (חַשְׁמַל) is the same as that of *Malbush* (מַלְבּוּשׁ), the Hebrew word for "garment."[40] (A general discussion of *Gematria* appears in a later section, where this particular one is worked out.)

From this discussion, we can also understand the account of Adam's sin on a somewhat deeper level.

When the serpent was tempting Eve, he said, "On the day that you eat of it . . . you shall be like God, knowing good and evil" (*Genesis 3:5*). On its surface, this is a very enigmatic statement. Equally puzzling is the question of how Adam and Eve, who possessed extraordinary intelligence, could have succumbed to the serpent's argument in the first place.

But as we discussed earlier, the goal of man's creation was that he should strive to imitate God. The serpent therefore argued that God Himself was the Creator of evil, and therefore He "knew good and evil." If Eve were to eat of the Tree of Knowledge, she, too, would "know good and evil," and in this way would resemble God. The serpent contended that in doing this, Eve would fulfill God's purpose in creation, since she would be imitating Him.

The fallacy in this argument, of course, was that God had specifically commanded man not to partake of the tree. One does not fulfill God's purpose by going against His expressed word.

This also explains another enigmatic passage in the same account.

After Adam had sinned and was punished, the Torah says, "God made leather garments for Adam and his wife, and He clothed them. And God said, 'Behold, man has become like one of us . . .'"(*Genesis 3:21,22*).

This last expression is most difficult to understand.

40 See notes 39 and 76.

What does God mean when He says, "Man has become like one of us"? This is especially difficult in light of the fact that man had just sinned and been punished. Even more enigmatic is the question of what this has to do with the fact that Adam and Eve had just been given clothing.

But God was saying that, now that man had sinned and was subject to evil thoughts, he needed a protection against evil. In this respect, he had become like God, who also wears a "garment" serving a similar purpose. Here again, however, this resemblance was not a positive one. What God actually wanted was that man resemble God in overcoming evil, and not that he should succumb to it and need to be protected against it.

The Tallith

We can now look into another question that people often ask. We know that the Torah contains 613 commandments, 248 do's and 365 don'ts. But why? Why is it necessary to have so many laws? Isn't it enough for people to have a general idea of what is right and then adhere to it?

There are many people today who argue that we should do away with laws completely. They say that all that is necessary is that people be good and love one another. They point out that at times laws can be harsh. Why then, did God give so many laws in the Torah?

The answer, of course, is because there is evil in the world. If men were perfect, then we would need few, if any, laws. People would live in total peace with one another, without any rules or regulations. This is indeed true of animals, who live in total harmony with other members of their species, without anything remotely resembling formal law. It is all part of their intrinsic nature.

The same was true of Adam before he sinned. He was innocent of any evil, and therefore did not need a multitude of rules and laws. All that was required was that he obey his one commandment not to eat of the Tree of Knowledge. That one commandment was enough to give him free will and thus enable him to achieve perfection and a closeness to God.[41] It was only after man sinned that he needed an entire complex of law.

The commandments therefore serve as a safeguard against the forces of evil. They restrict man's relationship with his neighbor so that one individual does not harm another. They constantly remind us of our obligation to God, so that we do not become swallowed up in evil.

We therefore see that to a large degree, the commandments of the Torah serve to protect us from evil. They are, in this respect, the element of God's plan that serves as a barrier against the forces of evil. This is what God meant when He said, "I have created the Evil Urge (*Yetzer HaRa*), but I have created the Torah as a remedy for it."[42]

The Torah's commandments are the element in God's scheme that serve as a barrier against evil. But, as we have discussed earlier, this is also the concept of God's "garment."

God's Tallith is therefore the sum total of all the commandments in the Torah. This is what our sages mean when they say, "He who keeps the commandments

---

[41] *Derekh HaShem* 1:3:6; *Adir BeMarom* (B'nai Brak, 5728) p. 11.
[42] *Kiddushin* 30b; *Bava Metzia* 16a.

grabs the Divine Presence. This is the meaning of Tzitzith . . ."[43]

As we shall see in the section on *Gematria*, the commandment of Tzitzith alludes to all 613 commandments. Our sages similarly teach us that, "The commandment of Tzitzith is equal to all the commandments."[44]

This is also what the Torah means when it speaks of the Tzitzith and says, "You shall see them and remember all of God's commandments, and not stray after your heart and after your eyes." The commandment of Tzitzith alludes to God's Tallith, which in turn, represents the entire structure of the commandments, standing as a barrier against evil.

After Adam sinned, the Torah says that, "They knew that they were naked, and they sewed together fig leaves and made themselves loincloths." There is a tradition that what they actually made were Tzitzith.[45] Rashi furthermore explains that when the Torah says, "They knew that they were naked," it means that they knew that they were naked "of the one commandment that God had given them."

As soon as man sinned, he realized that he would need the entire structure of commandments, alluded to in the Mitzvah of Tzitzith. As soon as he realized that he was naked of his one original commandment, he

---

[43] *Zohar* 1:23b. For the meaning of God's Tallith, see *Shaar HaKavanoth*, *Tzitzith* 2 (p. 28); *Pri Etz Chaim, Tzitzith* 3 (p. 68a). Also see *Tana DeBey Eliahu Zuta* 23 (51b); *Tikuney Zohar* 21 (55b); Bachya on Numbers 15:38; *Likutey Moharan* 8:8. For other explanations, see Rashba, *Berachoth* 6a; *Beer HaGolah* (Maharal) 4 (35b).

[44] See note 2, part 1.

[45] *Zohar* 1:28b. *Cf. Kli Yakar* on Numbers 15:38.

made himself Tzitzith, the one commandment that includes all the others.

The Midrash tells us that the first time that God is said to have appeared wearing a Tallith was when He gave Moses the first commandment, the one involving the Jewish calendar.[46] God was beginning to teach Moses the way of the commandments, and when He started, he showed Moses the Tallith that alludes to them all.

As mentioned earlier, one place in the Bible where God's Tallith is alluded to is in the verse, "He covers Himself with light as a garment" (*Psalms 104:2*). Here again, the allusion is to the light of the Torah and its commandments, as we find elsewhere, "A commandment is a lamp, and the Torah is light" (*Proverbs 6:23*).

Four Corners

The main element of God's plan that serves as a barrier against evil is the array of commandments in the Torah. But even though the commandments are Divine in origin, they do not serve their purpose unless they are fulfilled by man. In this sense, God's Tallith is not whole unless it is completed by man.

Man's role in completing God's garment of commandments is represented by the Tzitzith on the four corners of His Tallith.

In general, we know that the Tallith is only worn because of the Tzitzith that it contains. Without the Tzitzith, the Tallith is nothing more than a square piece of cloth. The same is true of God's Tallith. Unless ful-

---

[46] *Pesikta 5* (55a); *Pesikta Rabathai 15* (78a); *Yalkut 1:191; Rokeach 242* (p. 139).

filled by man, the commandments do not serve their purpose.

In this sense, the Tzitzith, being loose threads, are like the unwoven portion of the Tallith. As such, they represent the incompleteness in God's garment. This unwoven part is left for man to complete.[47]

The Tallith is therefore made in the form of a rectangle or square. Our sages teach us that a four-sided figure is the archetype of something that is manmade.[48] The square shape of the Tallith alludes to the fact that the main responsibility to complete God's Tallith lies in the hands of man.

The bond between God and man involves all levels of creation. Man is the goal of God's creation, and all the spiritual worlds exist only for his sake. There are essentially four levels in the spiritual plane, alluded to by the four letters in God's ineffable Name (יהוה, YHVH). The four corners of the Tallith allude to these levels, and thus, to the spiritual link between God and man.

In Ezekiel's vision, after he saw the *Chashmal*, which was God's "garment," he saw the four angels called *Chayoth*. These four angels are the four Tzitzith on the corners of God's Tallith.[49] This is why the prophet saw them attached to the *Chashmal*, which represents God's Tallith. Our sages furthermore teach us that the *Chashmal* exists primarily for these angels,[50] just as the Tallith

---

[47] *Meshech Chochmah* on Numbers 15:38.

[48] *Yerushalmi Nedarim* 3:2 (9a); *Bahir* 114, *Elemah Rabothai* (RaMaK) 1:4:14 (29b); *Avodath Yisroel* on Numbers 15:38.

[49] *Baal HaTurim*, Abarbanel, Bachya, on Numbers 15:38; *Targum Yonathan* on Numbers 15:40; *Zohar* 3:226b, 227a; *Tikuney Zohar* (10:25b).

[50] According to the Talmud (*Chagigah* 13b, top) the etymology of the word *Chashmal* is *Chayoth Esh Memalleloth*, or "*Chayoth* of Fire, speaking." Cf. *Zohar* 2:81b, 3:228a; *Tikuney Zohar* 19 (28b); *Shaar HaHakdamoth, Orchey HaKinuyim, Kaf* (p. 220).

is worn primarily for the Tzitzith that it contains. As we know, God's providence is directed primarily through these angels; therefore, they also represent the link between God and man.

Since the Tzitzith represent the bond between God and man, they hang down below the Tallith. God's Tallith is high above our reach, but His Tzitzith hang down like a lifeline that we can grasp hold of.[51] They reach down to us so that we may complete God's Tallith, while at the same time perfecting ourselves.

The Tzitzith therefore have five knots, representing the five books of the Torah. The Tzitzith begin with the knots, since the first step in bringing the commandments within man's reach is the Torah. These knots bind the Tzitzith to the Tallith, just as the Torah and its commandments bind man to God.[52]

The Eight Strings

There is a song that we sing on Passover night that teaches us many important lessons about numbers. You may have sung "Who Knows One?" (*Echad Mi Yodea*) many times, but have you ever thought of the significance behind the words? This song, in short, tells of the particular significance that each number has to the Jewish people.

When we ask "Who knows eight?" the song replies, "Eight days for circumcision." The particular significance of the number eight is the fact that the ritual of circumcision is always performed on the eighth day.

[51] Bachya on Numbers 15:38 (83c); *Noam Elimelech ibid. Cf. Zohar* 3:175b; *BeMidbar Rabbah* 17:9.
[52] *Likutey Halachoth, Netilath Yadayim* 4:11. *Cf. Zohar* 3:228b.

Circumcision—the *Brith* or Covenant—is the most ancient ritual of Judaism. It was the covenant that God made with Abraham as soon as he was chosen to be the father of the Jewish people. But what is its significance?

A major clue comes from the fact that circumcision is always performed on the eighth day. Let us stop for a moment and consider the significance of the number eight.

We all know that we live in a three-dimensional world. Our universe contains three dimensions, length, breadth and height. Take this a step further, and you see that each dimension has two directions. Therefore, there are a total of six primary directions in our physical world: up and down, right and left, forward and backward.

Rabbi Yehudah Löw (1525–1609), the famed Maharal of Prague, points out that this is one of the main reasons why the world was created in six days.[53] To complete a three-dimensional world, God spent six days, one for each primary direction.

The Maharal goes on to explain that this is also the reason for the Sabbath. We can think of the six primary directions as six lines, all emanating from a single central point. The Sabbath then represents this center point. As such, it is what connects the six directions, and thus unifies our three-dimensional world.

We can then see that the number seven represents the perfection of the physical world. In resting on the seventh day, God completed and perfected His creation, binding it all together with a central purpose. This is one reason why the number seven appears in so many places in Jewish lore.

[53] *Tifereth Yisrael* 40. Cf. *Sefer Yetzirah* 4:3.

But beyond the physical, there is the transcendental. What number pertains to this? What number do we use when we wish to transcend the physical completely? It should be obvious that this is the number eight.

A good example of this is the miracle of Chanukah. The fact that one night's supply of oil continued to burn was a miracle that transcended the mere laws of nature. We are dealing with a miracle that goes beyond the physical. For this reason Chanukah is an eight-day festival.

The same is true of the splitting of the Red Sea, the greatest miracle ever. This also took place on the eighth day of the drama that was the Exodus. As we know, one reason we celebrate the seventh day of Passover is that the Red Sea was split on that day. Since the Exodus actually began on the day before Passover, the splitting of the Red Sea was on the eighth day of this drama. Here again, this was because it was a miracle that transcended the mere physical.[54]

Circumcision is also performed on the eighth day, essentially for the same reason. Circumcision represents God's covenant with Abraham. Through this, God was establishing the fact that Abraham and his children would be living on a plane that would transcend the mere physical. From that time forward, the Jew would have a direct link to the spiritual realm.[55]

The fact that circumcision was to be performed on the sexual organ is also of particular significance. In the act of reproduction, man comes in contact with the

[54] For the relationship of this to Tzitzith, see Rashi on Numbers 15:41; *Sifsey Chachamim, Gur Aryeh,* Bachya *ad loc.* Also see Rashi, *Menachoth* 43b s.v. *Domeh Le Yam; Smag,* positive 26 (p. 109a).

[55] *Tifereth Yisrael* (Maharal) 1, 2. *Cf. VaYikra Rabbah* 27:10; *Derekh Mitzvothecha* (Chabad) 9b.

transcendental in a most unique way. Through the sexual act, one can begin the process of birth, thus drawing down a soul from the highest spiritual realm. The fact that the circumcision of the sexual organ is associated with the number eight is indicative of its link to the transcendental.

On a more mundane level, circumcision also serves as an indelible bodily sign, and a constant reminder that one must remain master of his sexual passions.[56] But, as we have seen, this is closely related to the former reason.

This is the significance of the eight strings of the Tzitzith.[57] They indicate that the Jew has a link with the transcendental. Through the commandments, man can achieve a unique relationship with God. The eight strings bind us to God's "garment," and they indicate that we are bound to something that goes far beyond the realm of the physical world.[58]

The eight strings are bound by the five knots, representing the five books of the Torah. The only link that the strings have with the Tallith is through the knots. This indicates that there is only one way to achieve the transcendental; that is through the five books of the Torah.

---

[56] Cf. *Moreh Nebukhim* 3:49.

[57] The eight strings allude to the eight days of circumcision, cf. Bachya on Numbers 15:38 (83a); *Menorath HaMaor* 3:3:4:3 (125).

[58] This is also the reason why the total number of strings on all four corners is 32, alluding to the 32 *Nesivoth Chochmah* (Paths of Wisdom). Cf. *Bahir* 92, *Zohar* 3:175a, 3:227a, 3:301a; Bachya on Numbers 15:38, Rekanti, *Shlach* 38c, Tzitzith 10a; *Reshith Chochmah, Shaar HaKedushah* 7 (141d); *Pardes Rimonim* 23:9; *Pri Etz Chaim,* Tzitzith 6 (p. 81); *Nahar Shalem* p. 71. For a general discussion of the 32 *Nisivoth,* see *Sefer Yetzira* 1:1 ff. Also see note 80.

There are a number of other important parallels between circumcision and Tzitzith.[59]

Most obvious is the fact that they both serve as a reminder that we must master our sexual infatuations. Less well known is the fact that they both ultimately originated with Abraham.[60] Regarding circumcision, God told Abraham, "This is My covenant . . . every male among you shall become circumcised . . . he that is eight days old shall be circumcised" (*Genesis 17:10,12*). The origin of Tzitzith with Abraham, however, is not as well known.

One of the important events in Abraham's career was his battle with the four kings, as described in the 14th chapter of Genesis. Although this was an actual battle, it also symbolized Abraham's fight against all the forces of evil in the world. After the battle, Abraham was blessed by Shem, son of Noah (Melchizedek), who declared, "Blessed be Abram of God Most High, Maker of heaven and earth" (*Genesis 14:19*). In conferring this blessing, Shem was also ordaining Abraham as the bearer of all the traditions that had been handed down from the times of Adam and Noah.[61]

Immediately after this, Abraham was invited to take his share of the spoil from the battle. His immediate reply was, "I have lifted my hands to the Lord, God Most High . . . that I will not take a thread or a shoe-lace . . ." (*Genesis 14:22,23*). Our sages teach us that because Abraham said, "I will not take a thread," his

---

[59] Tzitzith thus allude to *Yesod* (Foundation) the *Sefirah* associated with the reproductive organ, *cf. Tikuney Zohar* 21 (55b); *Pri Etz Chaim, Tzitzith* 2 (p. 66).

[60] *Menorath HaMaor* 3:3:4:3 (125).

[61] *Nedarim* 32b, Ran *ad loc.* s.v. *U'Malki Tzedek; Pirkey Rabbi Eliezer* 8 (18b); Radal *ad loc.* 8:17.

children were later given the thread of Tzitzith.[62]

The reason for this is the same as before. The eight threads of Tzitzith represent man's link with the transcendental. By disdaining all worldly gain—even as little as a thread—Abraham was demonstrating that his main interest was in the Godly and spiritual. His children were therefore worthy of Tzitzith, which are indicative of this link with the extra-mundane.

God's Attributes

If we go back to our song, "Who Knows One?" in the last stanza we find another number that is important to our discussion. That is the number 13. The song asks, "Who knows thirteen?" and replies, "Thirteen are the Attributes."

There are two definitions of these thirteen Attributes.

One reference is to the thirteen attributes or rules that our sages used to explain the Torah. You might recall seeing Rabbi Yishmael's enumeration of these thirteen rules in the prayer book, as part of the daily morning service.[63] The main purpose of these thirteen rules is to bring the general laws elucidated in the Torah down to the level of practical application.

The second reference here is to the Thirteen Attributes of God's mercy. These are the Attributes proclaimed by God when He forgave the Jews for the sin of the Golden Calf.

They are cited in the Torah, "God (1), merciful (2)

---

[62] *Sotah* 17a; *Chulin* 89a; *Bereshith Rabbah* 43:9; *Tanchuma, Lech Lecha* 13; *Zohar* 3:175b.

[63] Taken from the introduction to *Sifra* (*Torath Kohanim*), cf. *Tur Orach Chaim* 50. For the relationship between these and the Thirteen Attributes of Mercy, see *Zohar* 3:228a; *B'nai Yesas'char, Rosh Chodesh* 4:3, *Tamuz* 3:7.

and gracious (3), slow (4) to anger (5), and abundant in love (6) and truth (7). Keeping mercy (8) to the thousandth generation (9), forgiving sin (10), rebellion (11), and error (12), and cleansing (13)" (*Exodus 3:46*).[64]

Another place where these Thirteen Attributes appear is in the words of the Prophet, "Who is a God like you (1), who pardons sin (2) and overlooks rebellion (3) to the remnant of His heritage (4). He retains not His anger forever (5), for He desires mercy (6). He will again have mercy on us (7). He will subdue our sins (8), and cast all our errors in the depths of the sea (9). You will show truth to Jacob (10), love to Abraham (11), as sworn to our fathers (12) from days of old (13)" (*Micah 7:18–20*).[65]

The number thirteen, however, is also very important with respect to Tzitzith. Tzitzith contain five knots and eight strings, which together yield a total of thirteen. We will come across this again in our discussion of *Gematria*.[66]

This is related to both definitions of the thirteen Attributes given above. The Tzitzith represent God's link with man, and man's responsibility to complete God's Tallith. God's Tallith furthermore represents the sum total of the commandments.

God's Tallith, however, only represents the commandments in their most abstract form. Before they can be fulfilled by man, they must be applied to actual situ-

---

[64] *Etz Chaim, Shaar Arich Anpin* 9; *Zohar* 2:4b, 3:131b. Also see Rashi, Ibn Ezra, Ramban, *Baaley Tosafoth, Sforno ad loc.; Tosafoth Rosh HaShanah* 17b s.v. *Shalosh; Sefer Chasidim* 250; *Makor Chesed ad loc.* 250:3.

[65] *Zohar* 3:131b, *Etz Chaim ibid.; Tomer Devorah* 1.

[66] See note 75. The *Zohar*, however, speaks of thirteen *Chulyoth* or triplets that make up the 39 windings. See *Zohar* 3:227a; *Tikuney Zohar* 10 (25b).

ations. The rule used to apply the commandments to practical situations are precisely the thirteen principles through which the Torah is expounded. These are therefore represented by the Tzitzith, which link the abstract Tallith of God to the concrete problems of man. In this manner the thirteen knots and strings in the Tzitzith allude to the thirteen principles used in explaining the commandments.[67]

On a more abstract level, God's Tallith also represents His providence in protecting against evil. This element of providence, however, does more than just battle evil and protect us from it. Since it serves as the link between good and evil, it is the element that allows us to elevate evil and transform it into good. This is the concept of repentance. Despite the sin and evil a person may have done, a lifeline remains whereby he can repent and return to God. The vehicle of such forgiveness of sin is God's Thirteen Attributes of Mercy.

The five knots and eight strings of the Tzitzith also represent these Thirteen Attributes of Mercy.[68] Both represent the thread that links man to God's protection against evil. Through the Tzitzith of God's Tallith, an individual can pull himself out of the mire of sin and return to God.[69]

This brings us back to Rabbi Yochanan's statement, quoted at the beginning of this section. As you recall, Rabbi Yochanan said that, "God wrapped Himself [with a Tallith] like a prayer leader."

If we look at the context of this statement, we see that Rabbi Yochanan is speaking of the time when God for-

---

[67] *Zohar* 3:228a
[68] *Ibid.*
[69] *Likutey Halachoth, Tzitzith* 5:8.

gave Israel for the sin of the Golden Calf. God "wrapped Himself with a Tallith" precisely when he proclaimed the Thirteen Attributes of Mercy.

Rabbi Yochanan is teaching us that God wrapped Himself with a "Tallith;" the five knots and eight strings of His Tzitzith represented the Thirteen Attributes of Mercy that God was then proclaiming.[70]

There is a third way in which the number thirteen represents the bond between God and man. These are the thirteen special commandments that serve especially to bind us to God. They are:[71]

1. Belief in God.
2. Fear of God.
3. Love of god.
4. Belief in God's unity.
5. Study of Torah.
6. Wearing Tefillin.
7. Wearing Tzitzith.
8. Affixing the Mezuzah.
9. Circumcision.
10. Sabbath observance.
11. Prayer.
12. Festival observance.
13. The Sh'ma.

These are the thirteen commandments that serve as a particular bond between man and God. Of course, all the other commandments also bind man to God, but they do so in a more general manner. These thirteen commandments, however, are the ones that particularly serve this primary purpose; they, too, are represented

70 *Ibid.*
71 *Zohar* 3:257a.

by the five knots and eight strings of the Tzitzith.

From this, we can also begin to understand the reason there are 613 commandments. One major purpose of the commandments is to elevate all worldly things to the Godly.[72] This pertains particularly to the mundane things in the world, representing the six days of creation. We, therefore, have 600 commandments, one hundred for each day of creation.

In addition, we have the thirteen special commandments whose primary purpose is to link man to God. The total then is 613 commandments.[73]

[72] *BeMidbar Rabbah* 17:8. Note that this exposition is given with regard to Tzitzith in particular.

[73] *Zohar* 3:227a. The hundred commandments for each day are very much like the hundred blessings mentioned on *Menachoth* 43b. For another derivation of the number 613, see Rabbi Azriel on *Shir HaShirim*, quoted in Bachya on Numbers 15:38 (83b); *Reshith Chochmah, Shaar HaKedushah* 6 (142d).

NUMBERS

Do you know how to write Hebrew numbers? If you do, you probably know that classical Hebrew did not have separate number symbols, but represented them with a letter of the alphabet. It was a system something like the Roman numerals, but much simpler. The numerical value of letters of the Hebrew alphabet are given in the table following.

The fact that Hebrew uses letters instead of numerals opens a very interesting possibility. If each letter in a word represents a number, then the word as a whole must also have a numerical value. We refer to this when we speak of the numerical value, or *Gematria*, of a word.

Looking into it more deeply, we realize that there is an important reason for this relationship. As mentioned earlier, Hebrew is the Holy Tongue (*Lashon HaKodesh*), and even its linguistic structure can teach us important lessons.

In this case, the lesson is fairly clear. Both words and numbers convey information. In the case of words, this is obvious. A statement such as, "David eats bread," tells us something, and thus conveys information. We communicate with words, and through them, we convey information to one another.

Numbers also convey information. When I say $3 + 5 = 8$, I am making a statement of fact, very much like the statement, "Roses are red." I am telling you something, and thus communicating information. As you might know, we communicate with computers entirely by means of numbers and symbols. There is also an entire language of higher mathematics.

Although numbers communicate information, they do so in a much more abstract manner than words do. When I speak of the number three, it can equally well refer to three apples, three people, three nations, or three abstract concepts.

NUMERICAL VALUES OF LETTERS

Aleph	א	1	*Lamed*	ל	30
Beth	ב	2	*Mem*	מ	40
Gimel	ג	3	*Nun*	נ	50
Dalet	ד	4	*Samech*	ס	60
Heh	ה	5	*Eyin*	ע	70
Vav	ו	6	*Peh*	פ	80
Zayin	ז	7	*Tzadi*	צ	90
Cheth	ח	8	*Kof*	ק	100
Teth	ט	9	*Resh*	ר	200
Yod	י	10	*Shin*	ש	300
Kaf	כ	20	*Tav*	ת	400

We can therefore say that the numerical value or *Gematria* of a word conveys its more abstract connotations.[74] When two otherwise unrelated words have the

<hr/>

[74] Cf. *Likutey Amarim* (*Tanya*) 2:1 (77a).

same numerical value, we can expect them to be connected in an abstract sense, or on a higher spiritual level.

The link between numbers and words is a link between the abstract and the concrete. As we have seen, this is also the significance of Tzitzith. We might therefore expect numbers to play an important role in Tzitzith, and this is indeed the case. In our discussions, we have already spoken of four corners, five knots, eight strings, 39 windings, and 613 commandments. We have also noted that detailed measurements are important to Tzitzith, and there also, numbers are involved. As we shall now see, the numerical value of words also plays an important role in Tzitzith.

Our sages teach us that the numerical value of the word Tzitzith is 600. Taken together with the five knots and eight strings, this gives us 613, the total number of commandments. The Tzitzith thus remind us of "all of God's commandments."[75]

To get a feel for it, let us actually go through this *Gematria.* Taking the word Tzitzith (צִיצִית) we have:

צ	Tzadi	=	90
י	Yod	=	10
צ	Tzadi	=	90
י	Yod	=	10
ת	Tav	=	400
			600

[75] *BeMidbar Rabbah* 18:21; *Tanchuma, Korach* 12; *Zohar* 3:227a; *Rashi on Numbers* 15:39; *Abarbanel ibid.*; Rashi *Shevuoth* 29a, *Menachoth* 43b s.v. *Shekula*; Rabenu Gershom, *Menachoth* 41a, end; *Tosafoth Ibid.*, 39a s.v. *VeLo. Cf.* Ramban on Numbers 15:39, and on *Sefer HaMitzvoth, Shoresh* 1.

We see that in the abstract, the word Tzitzith alludes to the general commandments. These are the ones that serve as a link to God in an overall manner. The five knots and eight strings allude to the thirteen command-ments that particularly serve to bind us to God. This gives us the total of 613.

To take another example, in our discussion of the mysterious word *Chashmal* (חַשְׁמַל), we pointed out that it represented the elements of God's providence that protected against evil. We also mentioned that it was identical to God's "garment," because both *Chashmal* and *Malbush* (מַלְבּוּשׁ), the Hebrew word for garment, have the same numerical value.[76]

Let us now work this out. Taking both *Gematrios* simultaneously, we have:

Chashmal חַשְׁמַל				*Malbush* מַלְבּוּשׁ			
ח	Cheth	=	8	מ	Mem	=	40
שׁ	Shin	=	300	ל	Lamed	=	30
מ	Mem	=	40	ב	Beth	=	2
ל	Lamed	=	30	ו	Vav	=	6
			378	שׁ	Shin	=	300
							378

Another very important place where *Gematria* comes into play is in the case of the Tzitzith windings. As dis-cussed earlier, the windings allude to God's unity, which binds everything together. It is therefore custom-ary to make 39 windings, the numerical value of *Ha-shem Echad*—"God is One." Let us look at the *Gematria* in detail.[77]

[76] See above, note 39.

[77] *Perishah, Orach Chaim* 11:22; *Machtzith HaShekel* 11:22; *Ba'er Heteiv* 11:24; *Mishnah Berurah* 11:70. Also see *Shaar HaKavanoth, Tzitzith* 6

Hashem יהוה

י	Yud	=	10	
ה	Heh	=	5	
			15	15
ו	Vav	=	6	
ה	Heh	=	5	
			11	11
				26 26

Echad אחד

א	Aleph	=	1	
ח	Cheth	=	8	
ד	Dalet	=	4	
			13	13
				39

This *Gematria* immediately gives us the reason for the 39 windings. But if you look carefully at the subtotals, you will also see the reason for the number of windings in each group. Just as a reminder, the groups have 7, 8, 11 and 13 windings respectively.

The first group contains seven windings in accordance with the Talmudic injunction that no group contain less than this number.[78] As we discussed earlier, this represents the perfection of the physical world, which was created in seven days

The second group has eight windings, alluding to the transcendental.[79] Together, the first two groups have a total of 15 windings, the numerical value of the first two letters of God's Name.

The third group has eleven windings. This is the

(47a); *Yam Shel Sh'lomo, Yebamoth* 1:3; *Magen Avraham* 11:22.

[78] *Menachoth* 39a; *Tosafoth ad loc.* s.v. *Lo*; Raavad, *Tzitzith* 1:7; HaGra on *Orach Chaim* 11:14 s.v. *VeNohagin.*

[79] *Cf. Pri Megadim, Eshel Avraham* 11:22.

numerical value of the last two letters of God's Name. The first three groups thus have 26 windings, the total numerical value of God's Name.

Finally, the last group has thirteen windings. This is the maximum allowed in any group, and is also the numerical value of *Echad*, the Hebrew word for "one." This also alludes to the Thirteen Attributes, and the fact that this is the numerical value of *Echad*—one—indicates that these Attributes are all manifestations of God's ultimate unity.

The word *Echad* also alludes to the Tallith in another manner. *Echad* (אֶחָד) is spelled *Aleph, Cheth, Dalet.* Aleph (א) has the numerical value of one, alluding to the one Tallith containing the Tzitzith. Cheth (ח) is eight, representing the eight strings. Finally, *Dalet* (ד) is four, alluding to the four corners of the Tallith.

The final thing that we will examine in this section is sort of a reverse *Gematria*. As you now well know, each of the four Tzitzith has eight strings. This gives us a total of 32 strings on the four corners. The number 32, however, written in Hebrew is *Lamed Beth*—the letters that spell out *Lev* (לֵב), the Hebrew word for heart. Thus, the Tzitzith represent the heartstrings, constantly beating, yearning, and drawing one toward God.

[80] *Zohar* 3:175b; *Likutey Halachoth, Tzitzith* 1 (32b), 5:23. See *Baaley Tosafoth* on Numbers 15:38. Also see note 58.

A THREAD OF BLUE

You shall place on the Tzitzith of [each] corner a thread of blue . . .

A THREAD OF BLUE

Very often, people ask, "Where is the blue thread in the Tzitzith?"

We read the section dealing with Tzitzith twice daily in our prayers and each time, we read the words, "You shall place on the Tzitzith of [each] corner, a thread of blue." But when you look at the Tzitzith that people wear, you never seem to find this blue thread.

Of course, the stripes that are often put on the Tallith are supposed to allude to the blue thread,[1] but still, the thread itself is missing. If the Torah tells us to put a blue thread in the Tzitzith, why don't we do so?

Our sages teach us that adding the blue thread is preferable, but its absence does not invalidate the Tzitzith. Tzitzith made only with white threads are perfectly valid.[2]

The great commentator, Rabbi Moshe Alshech,

---

[1] *Pri Megadim, Mishbetzoth Zahav* 9:6; *Taamey HaMinhagim* 15.

[2] *Menachoth* 4:1 (38a); *Yad, Tzitzith* 1:4. However, see *HaMaor HaKatan, Shabbath* (Rif 11b), who holds that Tzitzith are not valid without the blue thread. See *Pri Megadim*, Introduction, s.v. *Tzitzith*; *Pethil Techeleth* 5 (p. 110).

explains that this is why the Torah says, "They should make Tzitzith on the corners of their garments *for all generations.*" The commandment of Tzitzith applies to all generations, even when there is no blue. Regarding the commandment of the blue thread, however, the Torah does not say "for generations." When the blue is available, it should be used; but if it is not available, this does not prevent us from fulfilling the commandment of Tzitzith.

We do not add the blue thread today because the art of dying it has been lost. This particular blue is known in the Torah as *Techeleth,* and according to tradition, can only be obtained from an animal known as the *Chilazon.*[3] Since we no longer know the precise identity of this animal, we cannot dye the blue thread properly.

Even in ancient times, not everybody wore the blue thread in his Tzitzith. The *Chilazon* was a very rare animal, and even a single thread of this blue wool was very expensive.[4] For this reason, there was a time when almost no one at all wore it in Jerusalem.[5]

With the destruction of the second Temple, (*Beth HaMikdash*), the supply of this particular blue dye virtually disappeared.[6] Still, a small supply was maintained by a handful of individuals who knew where to find the *Chilazon.*[7] It appears that the blue *Techeleth* dye was used to some extent until the eighth century

---

[3] *Tosefta, Menachoth* 9:6; *Shefuney Temuney Chol* 2 (p. 12). This requirement is questioned, however, in *Tifereth Yisrael.* Introduction to *Seder Moed, K'lelay Bigdey Kehunah* (p. 14b).

[4] *Menachoth* 44a.

[5] *Ibid.* 40a.

[6] *Cf. Shaar HaKavanoth, Tzitzith* 4 (p. 37), *Pri Etz Chaim, Tzitzith* 5 (p. 77).

[7] *Sifri* (354) on Deuteronomy 33:19.

c.e.[8] The city of Tyre was the center of the ancient dying industry, and it is probable that whatever blue dye was available during this period came from there. It is quite possible that the conquest of Tyre by the Moslems around this time dried up the supply of *Techeleth* completely.[9]

The blue thread used in the Tzitzith was a special color known as *Techeleth*. There appear to be, however, several opinions as to the precise shade of blue that was used. According to the Rambam (Maimonides), it was the color of a clear noon sky,[10] similar to a pale indigo.[11] Rashi, on the other hand, writes that it was the color of

---

[8] From Raavad, *Tzitzith* 1:7, it would appear that Rav Natrunai Gaon, who died in 761 c.e., still had *Techeleth* (*Seder HaDoroth* p. 69a, *Shalsheleth HaKabalah* 36b). *Cf. Shefuney Temuney Chol* p. 9. It also appears that Rabbi Shimon Kiira, author of *Halachoth Gedoloth* also had *Techeleth cf. HaMaor HaKatan loc. cit.*, and he, too, lived between 678 and 703 c.e. See *Pethil Techeleth*, p. 44. The earliest statement regarding the absence of *Techeleth* appears in *BeMidbar Rabbah*, 17:8; *Tanchuma Shlach* 15; but see *Shefuney Temuney Chol* p. 9. Also see Rambam on *Menachoth* 4:1; *Sefer HaChinukh* 386; *Rokeach* #361 (p. 247); HaGra on *Orach Chaim* 9:1.

[9] *Pethil Techeleth* p. 44. *Cf. Shabbath* 26a, that this dye came from Tyre.

[10] *Yad, Tzitzith* 2:1, *Kley HaMikdash* 8:13. In his commentary on *Berakhoth* 2:1, *Kelayim* 9:1, the Rambam writes that it is like the color of *Tarshish*, the precious stone mentioned in Exodus 28:29. See *Chulin* 91b, Rashi *ad loc. s.v. VeGeviasi*; Rabenu Gershom *ibid.*, that this is a Mediterranean blue. See *BeMidbar Rabbah* 2:7.

[11] The Rambam indicates that this is similar in color to *Isatis; Yad, Tzitzith* 2:1, Rambam on *Shevi'ith* 7:1, *Megillah* 4:7. This is most probably *Isatis Tinctoria* or Woad, a well known plant that produces a blue dye. In his commentary on *Kelayim* 2:5, however, the Rambam identifies this with the color of *Techeleth*, and states that it is Indi[go]. On *Shabbath* 9:5, he furthermore states that *Isatis* is skyblue. We also find in the Talmud that *Techeleth* resembled a dye known as *Kla Ilan*, *cf. Menachoth* 41b, *Baba Metzia* 41b. According to the *Arukh s.v. Kla* and the *Nimukey Yosef* (on *Baba Metzia*, Rif 34a *s.v. Ilan*) this *Kla Ilan* is indigo. (See Michael Sachs, *Beitrage zur Shprach und Alterthumsforshang*, Berlin 1852, 1:132, who identifies this with the Greek *Callainum*.) Also see *Tosafoth Chulin* 47b *s.v. Eleh*; Rabenu Yonah, *Berakhoth* (Rif 4b) *s.v. Rabbi Eliezer.*

the evening sky,[12] closer to a greenish blue or aquamarine.[13] Later authorities asserted that it was a dark grey-blue.[14]

Just any blue dye could not be used for the blue thread of Tzitzith. It had to be a special dye that came from an animal known as the *Chilazon*. There is no continuous tradition regarding the identity of the *Chilazon*, but according to most sources, it was a snail[15] that lived in the Mediterranean between Tyre and Haifa.[16] Our sages state that it is a boneless invertebrate,[17] and that, "When the *Chilazon* grows, its shell grows with

---

[12] Rashi on Numbers 14:41.

[13] Rashi, *Sotah* 17a s.v. *SheHa Techeleth* writes that it is not exactly the color of the sky, but more the color of the sea. In a number of other places, Rashi writes that *Techeleth* is *Yarok* or green; cf. Rashi on Exodus 25:4, Numbers 15:33, *Berachoth* 9b s.v. *Techeleth, Gittin* 31b s.v. *Sarbala.* From *Yerushalmi, Berakhoth* 1:2 (7b), it also appears that it has a greenish color, cf. *Marah HaPanim ad loc.* s.v. *Magid, Tosafoth, Sukkah* 31b s.v. *HaYarok, Chulin* 37b s.v. *Eleh.* See *BeMidbar Rabbah* 14:3; *Midrash Tehillim* 24:12.

[14] Rabbi Gershon Henoch of Radzin, *Shefuney Temuney Chol* 3 (p. 36); *Pethil Techeleth* 2 (p. 65); *Eyn Techeleth* 26 (p. 126), all in *Shlosha Sifrey Techeleth,* Jerusalem 5723.

[15] *Aruch* s.v. *Chilazon; Tifereth Yisrael,* Introduction to *Seder Moed, K'laley Bigdey Kehunah* p. 14b. *Chidushey HaRan, Shabbath* 107a (14:1), speaks of "our *Chilazons* who inhabit garbage heaps," most probably referring to the common European land snails. Also see *Eyn Techeleth* 20 (p. 115).

[16] *Shabbath* 26a, *Sifri loc. cit.* The Rambam in *Yad, Tzitzith* 2:2, writes that it is found in the "Salt Sea," but the reference is not to the Dead Sea, but to salt water in general, cf. Rambam on *Kelim* 15:1, *Tshuvoth Rambam* 154. Also see *Maadney Yom Tov,* Rosh, *Kelai Begadim* (after *Niddah*) 7:10; Radal on *Pirkey Rabbi Eliezer* 18:45, notes 6 and 7; *Torah Temimah* on Numbers 15:38 #118; *Shefuney Temuney Chol* p. 28; *Pethil Techeleth.* It occasionally emerges on mountains near the sea, cf. *Sanhedrin* 91a; Rashi, *Megillah* 6a s.v. *Al Yedey; Chulin* 89a; *T'shuvoth Radbaz* 685. It was also found in Italy, cf. *Targum* on Ezekiel 27:7.

[17] *Yerushalmi Shabbath* 1:3 (8a), *Korban HaEdah, P'nai Mosheh, ad loc.* s.v. *VeHalo Chilazon.* Also see *Tosafoth Shabbath* 73b s.v. *MeFarek;* Ritva, *Shabbath* 107a (14:1).

it."[18] There are also illusions to the fact that it has two feelers[19] and a snakelike body.[20] We also know that the animal itself was blue in color.[21]

The fact that the *Chilazon* can be identified with a species of snail is not at all surprising. It is well known that a number of snails played an important role in yielding the beautiful blue and purple dyes that made Tyre famous in ancient times. Of particular importance were the conchlike snails of the Murex and the Purpura families. Even today, fine dyes can be obtained from such species as the Purple Shell (*Murex trunculus, Murex brandaris, Purpurea patula*), the Purple Whelk (*Purpurea lapillus*), and the Purple Fish (*Murex purpurea*). All of these produce a purple or blue dye by means of special glands at the roof of their gill cavity.[22]

It is interesting to note that a number of our great sages have identified the *Chilazon* as the Purple Shell or Purpura.[23] This is a fairly large carnivorous Mediterranean snail, distinguished by a blue or purple shell containing rather large spines. It yields a creamy white fluid that turns purple when exposed to light. When mixed with soda, sea water and other chemicals, various shades of blue can be obtained from it.

---

[18] *Devarim Rabbah* 7:11; *Shir HaShirim Rabbah* 7:11; *Pesikta* 10 (92a); *Midrash Tehillim* 23:4; *Yalkut* 1:850, 2:691.

[19] *Kelim* 12:1; *Rosh ad loc.* s.v. *Chilazon, Shefuney Temuney Chol* 2:5.

[20] *Bekhoroth* 6:2 (38a), *Targum Yonathan*; Rashi, on Leviticus 21:20. *Cf. Shefuney Temuney Chol* 2:6.

[21] *Menachoth* 44a; *Shefuney Temuney Chol* 2:1.

[22] And therefore, it is not actually blood, cf. *Tosafoth, Shabbath* 75a s.v. *Ki; Shefuney Temuney Chol* 2:9.

[23] Ravya on *Berakhoth* 3b, quoted in *Torathan Shel Rishonim, Yerushalmi Berakhoth* 1:2, who states that *Techeleth* is *Pirpiron* or Purpura. The *Tifereth Yisrael loc. cit.* also identifies it as the "Purple Snail," quoting Wilhelm Gesenius, *Habräishes und chaldäishes Hanawörtbuch Uber dos Alte Testament* (1812).

There is, however, another important opinion regarding the identity of the *Chilazon,* and this involves a fascinating modern story.

One of the greatest European rabbis of the last century was Rabbi Gershon Henoch Leiner (1839–1890), of Radzin, Poland. By the age of thirteen, he was already a Talmudic scholar of repute, and for his Bar Mitzvah, he delivered a discourse that dazzled the leading rabbis of Europe. He was accepted as rabbi of Radzin at a young age, and before he was thirty, he had already published his *Sidrey Taharoth* (Order of Purity), one of the greatest works ever written on the complex laws of ritual purity.

In 1887, Rabbi Gershon Henoch set out on a new quest—to rediscover the identity of the *Chilazon,* the animal used to dye the blue in the Tzitzith. Utilizing his encyclopedic knowledge of all Judaic literature, he wrote a small pamphlet, *Shefuney Temuney Chol* (Hidden Treasures of the Sand), exploring all the Talmudic and Midrashic traditions regarding the *Chilazon.* On the basis of this research, he felt certain that he would recognize the animal if he saw it.

The Rabbi was not content merely to search in books, and he began a year-long pilgrimage to various ports to try to find the *Chilazon* in the flesh. His search finally led him to the world famous aquarium in Naples, Italy. Like a fascinated child, he gazed at the many tanks, looking for a creature that would satisfy all the necessary criteria. Finally, he found an animal that he believed to be the *Chilazon.*[24]

The creature that he discovered was the common

---

[24] The story of the search and discovery are to be found in the introductions to *Pethil Techeleth* and *Eyn Techeleth* (p. 29).

cuttlefish (*Sepia officinalis*), a member of the octopus family. His identification was so precise that he even provides us with the animal's Latin name. It is well known that the cuttlefish exudes a blue-black ink when frightened or attacked, and this has long been used to make a brown dye known as sepia. Rabbi Gershon Henoch experimented with the raw blue-black dye, and found that it would impart a dark blue color to wool. This, along with a number of other criteria, convinced him that the cuttlefish was the lost *Chilazon*.

From his own words, it is clear how excited the rabbi was with his discovery. He could reinstate a Mitzvah that had not been practiced for over a thousand years. He then wrote another book, *Pethil Techeleth* (A Thread of Blue), telling of his discovery. Since the usual codes of Jewish Law omit the details of how the fish is to be used, he included in his book a complete codification of these rules. He was now ready to introduce his discovery to the community at large.

By late 1889, the Rabbi had set up facilities for a rather large scale production of his blue wool, and within the course of a year, close to fifteen thousand people were wearing it in their Tzitzith. Since Rabbi Gershon Henoch was close to the Polish followers of Rabbi Nachman of Breslov, many of them also began to wear his blue.

All this did not go unnoticed by the other European rabbis, and many of them actively opposed this innovation. Correspondence ranged far and wide, disputing Rabbi Gershon Henoch's evidence. In response to this criticism, he wrote a third book on the subject, *Eyn HaTecheleth* (The Color of Blue), attempting to answer all those objections. Meanwhile, more and more people were wearing the blue, and it seemed as if it would finally take hold.

The movement came to an untimely halt, however, for on December 17, 1890 (4 Teveth, 5651), Rabbi Gershon Henoch passed away. Without his energetic leadership, the *Techeleth* movement died with him. Only his own followers and a small group of Breslover Chasidim continued to wear the blue thread. Less than a decade after his death, the author of the *Aruch HaShulchan* was able to write that an attempt to reintroduce the blue had been made, but it had not been accepted by the community at large.[25]

Although we do not wear the blue, it is interesting to note how it was worn during the brief period when it enjoyed a rennaissance. Most of the people who wore *Techeleth* followed the opinion codified by Rabbi Gershon Henoch.

There are three major opinions regarding the number of blue threads that were worn in Tzitzith.

The Rambam (Maimonides, 1135–1204) maintained that only half a string was dyed, so that just one of the eight strings was blue. This opinion was also accepted by the Kabbalists.[26]

The Raavad (Rabbi Avraham ben David of Posquieres, 1123–1198) held that an entire string was dyed, so that when doubled, two of the eight strings were blue.[27]

Finally, Rashi maintains that the blue and white were

[25] *Aruch HaShulchan* 9:12. For a discussion of some of the arguments raised against Rabbi Gershon Henoch's thesis, see *Shulchan Melachim* (*Shaarey Shalom*), *Pethicha LeHilkhoth Tzitzith* 5 (pp. 210a ff.)

[26] *Yad, Tzitzith* 1:6, *Kesef Mishneh ad loc.*; *P'er HaDor (Tshuvoth HaRambam)* 21. Also see *Shaar HaKavanoth, Tzitzith* 4 (p. 39); *Pri Etz Chaim, Tzitzith* 4 (p. 75).

[27] Raavad, *Tzitzith* 1:6. *Cf. Arukh* s.v. *Techeleth; Smag*, positive 26.

equal, two threads of each, so when doubled, four threads were blue, and four white.[28]

Rabbi Gershon Henoch felt inadequate to decide among these giants but since the Kabbalists agreed with the Rambam, he personally accepted this view.[29] He also wrote that the windings should be made exactly as we make them with all white threads, with one exception. Since he was now using the blue, the rule that the windings had to be subdivided into triplets (*Chulyoth*) had to be observed.[30] The first and last windings were made with a white thread, while all the others were blue.[31]

We do not follow Rabbi Gershon Henoch's opinion, but the story teaches us a very important lesson. The blue is not required for the Tzitzith, and they are perfectly valid without it. The most that the rabbi could accomplish was to provide a more perfect manner of observing this commandment. Even so, the rabbi and thousands of his followers spared neither expense nor effort in obtaining this blue dye.

We thus see how priceless this observance was to our ancestors. A mere thread—but of infinite value.

[28] Rashi, *Menachoth* 38a s.v. *HaTecheleth, Shabbath* 27b s.v. *Salka Daata Amina KeDeRaba; Tosafoth, Menachoth* 38a s.v. *HaTecheleth.*

[29] *Pethil Techeleth* p. 144.

[30] *Menachoth* 39a; *Yad, Tzitzith* 1:7; *Pethil Techeleth* p. 204.

[31] *Ibid.; Menachoth* 38b.